# the homiletical plot

## THE SERMON AS NARRATIVE ART FORM

### Eugene L. Lowry

John Knox Press
ATLANTA

The Scripture quotations in this publication are from the Revised Standard Version Bible, copyright 1946, 1952, and © 1971 by the Division of Christian Education, National Council of the Churches of Christ in the U.S.A. and used by permission.

Acknowledgment is made for permission to quote from the following:
From *As One Without Authority* by Fred B. Craddock. Copyright assigned © 1978 to Abingdon. Used by permission.

From "The Homiletical Bind" by Eugene L. Lowry. Copyright 1975 Christian Century Foundation. Reprinted by permission from the January 1975 issue of *The Christian Ministry*.

**Library of Congress Cataloging in Publication Data**

Lowry, Eugene L
    The homiletical plot.

    Includes bibliographical references.
    1. Preaching. I. Title.
BV4211.2.L68      251      80–15811
ISBN 0–8042–1652–5 (pbk.)

# contents

91410

To
Sarah

# introduction

There seems to be a wide disparity between "good preaching" as described formally and theoretically, and what happens on Sunday morning when we leave the pulpit with that certain interior knowledge that our sermon "was a good one." Likely as not we know we violated the "rules" of preaching theory we were taught (or are now learning); yet it happened. The story got told.

We wish we knew what it was precisely that made it happen. Not being able to identify what it is we do when we do well, we are left to happenstance. As Michael Polanyi, the philosopher, describes it: "We know more than we can tell."[1] If we could just transform our intuitions into articulate form regarding what it is that happens in our best preaching, we could *cause* it to happen by design.

*Transforming our intuitions into articulate form* is precisely the purpose of this book. In order to accomplish this task two things are necessary. First, we have to lay aside—at least temporarily—many of the cherished norms about sermon anatomy. For example, most books on preaching operate on the common assumption that sermonic organization evolves out of the logic of content. That is, one takes a theme or topic and cuts it up into equal parts (generally three), and then organizes the parts into some kind of logical order. As such the sermon looks like a "paste-up" even before it appears in the pulpit. We do this because that's the way we were taught. Even prior to seminary we were taught this way in speech class.

More crucially (and sub-consciously) our language system teaches us to think this way. So we have been taught the science of sermon *construction* as though we are a strange breed of architectural engineers. This way of thinking and organizing is one of the "cherished norms" we need to lay aside or even engage in battle. But that's not all!

We need also to form a new image of the sermon—one that is congruent with our best preaching. Truth is, to continue our example, a sermon is not a doctrinal lecture. It is an *event-in-time*, a narrative art form more akin to a play or novel in shape than to a book. Hence we are not engineering scientists; we are narrative artists by professional function.

Does it not seem strange to you that in our speech and homiletical training we seldom considered the connection between our work and that of the playwright, novelist or television writer? This is most remarkable when you consider that our best preaching does in fact feel like a story. It is indeed *The Story*, and our task is to tell it, to form it, to fashion it—not to "organize" it.

My hope is that whether you are a seminary student just learning the art of preaching and looking for something beyond mechanical rules, or are a seasoned practitioner, perhaps bored and burdened by the regular onslaught on Sunday morning sermon demands, you will find here a new vision of our common task.

I propose that we begin by regarding the sermon as a homiletical plot, a narrative art form, a sacred story.

# SECTION ONE
## the sermon as narrative

Reading a textbook on how to prepare sermons often is like looking up a word in a dictionary in order to find out how to spell it—you have to have the answer before you can probe the question! So it is that much homiletical advice tends to function in reverse—that is, it works reasonably well in evaluating a sermon already formed, but provides very little help *en route*! We are told, for example, that a good sermon is one that will "command the active attention of every listener." Fine, but you can't tell until it's too late! The dean of homiletical theorists, H. Grady Davis, suggests that a good sermon idea is one which is "generative"[1]—that is, one which has natural unfolding power. Most of us know exactly what he means—*after* we see one! But how do you get one?

How to find a "generative idea" is indeed both "first and foremost"—first because that is where we begin in preparing a sermon, and foremost because once the idea is found, the rest of the sermon preparation is easy by comparison. But the question of how to find a generative idea actually involves two quite distinct issues.

The first has to do with how to get started in preparing a sermon. What is going on inside my mind as I pace the floor of my study, trying to get started? What are the dynamics which mark the extraordinary transition from generalized or fragmented "Sunday morning thoughts" into that intuitively felt sense of having something that is alive and ready to be shaped?

The other issue is even tougher: What is the *form* of a homiletical idea? Would I recognize a generative idea if I found one? I am not asking the question of the *subject* or *topic* of some particular sermon. I am asking about the peculiar characteristic *form* that any subject takes when turned into a sermon. Obviously this question of homiletical form is preliminary to the other because until we resolve the issue of form, it is fruitless to ask how one begins to work toward it.

# the image of the sermon

All of us have an image of what a sermon is—that is, what factors characterize homiletical form. We learned it automatically, just by being alive and being in church. We do not think *about* this image—we just use it. So quite unconsciously it shapes what we do and how we do it.

For example, we take our language for granted. We do not stop to consider the fact that our language has individual letters that are collected into words, and words into phrases and phrases into sentences, etc. We just do it that way—and presume everyone else does too. But everyone else doesn't! (For example, many languages such as Chinese use pictures or ideograms instead of letters.) And those who do it differently, think differently.

Our language process of collecting little parts into bigger pieces until there emerges an organized whole is described by McLuhan as "the all-pervasive technology of the alphabet."[2] Considering the impact of the grammar of our "mother tongue," J. Samuel Bois, the general semanticist, observes that "we see the world through the meshes of that man-made filter."[3] Says Benjamin Whorf, the linguist:

> Each language is not merely a reproducing instrument for voicing ideas, but rather is itself a shaper of ideas. . . . We cut up nature, organize it into concepts, and ascribe significance as we do largely because we are parties to an agreement to organize it this way.[4]

Now what does this have to do with our image of a sermon? A glance at our preparation for last Sunday's sermon will perhaps reveal the answer. In all probability most of us started with scraps of notes—all generally related to a particular theme we hoped to mold into a sermon. And most of us made the same assumption—that if we could just properly organize the scraps of notes, there would emerge an integral whole called a sermon. That's the way we put together our sentences grammatically; that surely must be the way to organize a sermon. Well known to every preacher is the process of looking at a set of preliminary notes and asking "What could I put there?" or "I wonder if an illustration would flesh out this section?" The picture that emerges is that of an amateur carpenter who keeps adding braces here and there to steady a wobbly piece of work. Apparently a similar image occurred to Davis when he noted that this approach produces the "doghouse" sermon.[5] But the problem is not that we are amateurs and with a little practice will master the process. It is that the whole schema is born of an image of sermon-building as *assemblage* which is founded upon our unconscious understanding of reality as meaningfully related pieces. This is the automatic, and I believe, unfortunate "gift" our language system brings to our sermon work. It is as natural a consequence as is the fact that the industrial revolution with its mass production techniques relying on interchangeable parts is also a phenomenon born in the Graeco-Roman language world. The similarity between Henry Ford's worker reaching for interchangeable nuts and bolts with which to construct a car and the preacher reaching for interchangeable anecdotes and biblical proof-texts with which to construct a sermon is noteworthy.

In short we have been trained to see the sermon as a *thing*, and hence sermonic formation typically has consisted of organizing the constituent ingredients. The pervasiveness of this image of the sermon can be illustrated by noting what it is that we see in the following illustration. Most of us "see" an incompleted wall—a wall made of bricks or blocks. Our education and language have taught us to see this way, but in a literal (and perhaps banal) sense the illustration doesn't show bricks at all; it shows the mortar—but we tend not to see the connectives.

So likewise, our typical college speech and seminary preaching courses taught us to see things in certain ways—and hence not in other ways. Recall that very likely the emphasis regarding organization was upon the principles of outlining. I remember the lectures on how the various sub-points needed to be parallel to each other and equally subservient to the larger point, etc.[6] The entire matter is parallel to the above picture and how we saw it. To look at any outline is to look at a blueprint of organized ideas (a completed wall)—all fit together by a part-to-whole logic. The underlying mentality of such outlining instructions causes the *organizer* to focus upon the *substance* of the various points, but not upon the *transitions* which are the key to sermonic process. It is almost inevitable that we will concentrate on bricks and not notice the mortar.

In his excellent book *As One Without Authority*, Fred Craddock notes the difficulty experienced when trying to preach from such an outline, and asks:

> How does one get from 2b to main point II? That is a gulf that can be smoothly negotiated only by the most clever. Looked at geographically, a three-point sermon on this pattern would take the congregation on three trips down hill, but who gets them to the top each time? The limp phrase, "Now in the second place" hardly has the leverage. He who has had the nerve to cast a critical eye on his old sermons has probably discovered that some sermons were three sermonettes barely glued together. There may have been movement within each point, and there may have been some general kinship among the points, but there was not one movement from beginning to end. The points were as three pegs in a board, equal in height and distance from each other.[7]

The fact of "three pegs" serves notice that almost without fail this mentality will see substance, not movement (and will revere nouns

over verbs). This viewpoint will impel us toward organizing sermons on the basis of the logic of their ideational ingredients. But a
sermon is not a logical assemblage; a sermon is an event-in-time
which follows the logic born of the communication interaction between preacher and congregation. To organize on the basis of the
logic of ideational ingredients is to miss altogether the dynamics of
that communicational reality. (Imagine what the Prodigal Son story
would have been like had Jesus organized the message on the basis
of its logical ingredients instead of the journey of the son.)

In preaching seminars I ask participants to play a word association game with two terms: *construct* and *develop*. The composite
picture that emerges from words associated with "construct" is that
of a building site with pieces of lumber, bricks, iron, etc., off to the
side of a hole in the ground, with a hard-hatted man standing next
to a small building with a set of blueprints in his hand. He is an
engineer and his task is to put the pieces together according to the
plan drawn by an architect whose expertise is to know how to design buildings that will actually stand up (science) and in such a way
as to make the pieces look like they belong together (art).

The composite picture that emerges from words associated with
"develop" is something more akin to a several-time double-exposed
picture of a rose blossoming. The words used in this case more
often than not are words referring to living organic matter (such as
"grow," "form," "mature," etc.).

Note that the term "construct" evokes parts-to-whole expres-
sions and "develop" evokes terms associated with living matter processes not separable into distinct parts. This striking difference of
evoked association with the two terms is the difference between a
static collection of inanimate parts put together to look like a whole
on the one hand, and on the other, an organic living whole which is
not divisible.

Certainly I can tell the difference between a sermon I "constructed" and one which I "developed"! Sometimes a sermon idea
seemed to emerge on its own, possessed of its own power, and re-
quired a developmental process more akin to *pruning* than *putting
together*. Such an idea, says Grady Davis, "produces the sermon by
the energy, the vitality inherent in it."[8] Like a tree, he continues,

its branches are "thrust out by the force of its inner life."[9] Generally, with such a sermon idea I have more than enough material and do not find myself adding here and there. Rather, the task is to shape the idea in such a manner as to keep its direction appropriately focused and its integrity from becoming diffused.

I used to feel guilty about the sermon which seemed to have its own demands and desires. Its flow and movement just would not be restricted to three points, and I knew I was violating the principles of sermon making I had been taught! Yet this organic developmental kind of sermon took less preparation time, and it "preached" better.

Precisely the point! Of course I was violating the rules of sermon making—for many years before I had been taught the engineering science of sermon construction! To change the metaphor, I had been taught sermonic architecture (science), had learned to organize the pieces, and had hoped the parts would look like they belonged together (art). They seldom did! No wonder I then began deviating from my traditional instructions. In the midst of feeling guilty about my new style of forming sermons I began to ask if perhaps the problem was not so much my deviations but rather the instructions, the theories themselves.

Apparently others have had the same experience. Craddock notes that sometimes preachers who have prepared outlines for sermons will depart from them during the actual preaching experiences:

> Some have even felt guilty about the departure, feeling they had ceased preaching and had begun to "talk with" their people. Lacking a clearly formed alternative, shabby habits, undisciplined and random remarks have been the result of this groping after a method more natural and appropriate to the speaker-hearer relationship that prevails today. Such casual and rambling comments that have replaced the traditional sermon can hardly be embraced as quality preaching, but the instincts prompting the maneuver are correct.[10]

My conclusion is that a sermon ought not be a collection of parts constructed by a preacher, regardless of how we have been taught to think it so. The sermon has its roots in the truth of the gospel which indeed has a life of its own. Our task is the same as that of any artist whose act of discovery, as Eliseo Vivas describes it, is to "extricate the import and order of his experience and body it forth in language."[11] Calling the poet a "mid-wife"[12] Vivas explains that:

> The creative process thus involves a search for language [and form] that adequately captures in and through itself the object that, somehow, until it is successfully captured by language, lies tantalizingly just beyond the reach of consciousness.[13]

Our task in preaching is to facilitate the homiletical birth and development of such an idea grounded in the gospel. Rather than feeling guilty about violating the rules we once learned, we could bring judgment on these principles, recognizing that they are born of a mechanical image of reality. Rather than perceiving ourselves as engineers or architects, we view preaching as an art form and see ourselves as artists. We may be amateur artists or poor artists—but inescapably artists. What is needed badly is a different image of the sermon—one which can do justice to the developmental nature of the homiletical process. If our task is not to assemble parts but to facilitate a process, is there another image which might help us learn better how to do it?

Anyone who has happened to notice that the parable of the Prodigal Son is easier to handle homiletically than I Corinthians 13, or that often it is easier to preach from the Old Testament than the New, is not far from discovering another image of the sermon. The reason many Old Testament passages are more easily translatable into homiletical form is that the Hebrew language is a verb-based language and utilizes fewer adjectives and adverbs. Says Robert Roth in *Story and Reality*: "For the Greeks . . . words were definitions. . . . For the Hebrews, on the contrary, words were descriptions."[14] Hence there is more action or natural movement in *describing*, for example, a God who walks in the garden in the cool of the day than in *defining* a pre-existent Logos. Both the Prodigal Son narrative and I Corinthians deal with the qualities of love, but Jesus' parable uses story form to describe it by means of a father who "had compassion and ran and embraced him and kissed him" (Luke 15:20) while Paul defines it with the adjectives of "patient and kind" (I Cor. 13:4). Says Roth: "Stories begin once upon a time.

They move through episodes to a climax and then come to an end. . . . Stories move. *They have a plot.*"[15] (Italics mine.)

Suppose we were to ask a playwright to describe what would constitute an idea in that field. The answer would be: "Plot." A drama is an observed process in which a basic discrepancy or tension obtains resolution. The playwright sets us in the middle of an issue which "demands" some kind of remedy. "Propositions with subjects and predicates enter into these stories in an ancillary way," notes Roth, "but meaning arises from the experience of personal involvement in the dramatic action."[16]

Likewise, a sermon is a plot (premeditated by the preacher) which has as its key ingredient a sensed discrepancy, a homiletical bind. Something is "up in the air"—an issue not resolved. Like any good storyteller, the preacher's task is to "bring the folks home"— that is, resolve matters in the light of the gospel and in the presence of the people.

Plot! This is the key term for a reshaped image of the sermon. Preaching is storytelling. A sermon is a narrative art form.

In the introduction to his book of modern parables, G. William Jones notes the difference between the story and propositional statement:

> The usual tendency for going about this process [of preaching] comes much more from our Greek progenitors than from our Semitic progenitors. In order to head off all possibilities for misunderstanding, to make the message as "clear" as possible, we shuck it of its lifelike, experiential wrappings and lay it out as an abstract, propositional statement.[17]

On the other hand:

> there is almost always a sudden change whenever the speaker launches into a narrative. The audience becomes suddenly quiet, forgetting even to cough, sniff, or squirm, as the tale is spun. When they understand that it is over (and that now the speaker will draw his moral, make important announcements, etc.), the change back to coughing, sniffing, and squirming is equally as sudden.
> Actually, it hardly matters what kind of story, how good, how funny it is, how moving it is, or how well it is told. There is something almost automatically captivating about a

story that catches our minds and makes us forget to breathe until it is over.[18]

But his sharp delineation between story and "regular" preaching is unnecessary. Why not conceive *every* sermon as *narrative*—whether or not a parable or other story is involved? Remembering back to that sermon of yours that really went well: Is it not true that the key to its success had something to do with the terms "plot" and/or "narrative"? Perhaps it was that you put aside your carefully organized notes and simply "talked with the people." You began wrestling with the issue *with* them. You moved from what Jones calls "propositional statement" into story. (Note I did not say *a* story.)

Although Grady Davis probably did not intend it so, I believe this is the underlying truth of his statement that "the proper design of a sermon is the design of a time-continuity. And so I shall prefer to speak of the *continuity* or the *movement* of a sermon, rather than of its outline."[19] The terms "continuity" and "movement" in fact describe a narrative plot. The working through of a sensed discrepancy is what gives a sermonic idea its expansive or generative power.

Recall if you will when you first felt a homiletical idea "happen" to you. There was an excitement you felt, a tension which took hold. And you *knew* even before the sermon was formed, that you had it! At that time the tension perhaps was only latent to the actual sermon, but the tension was evidence of a discrepancy perhaps known only implicitly. In whatever way the sermon worked itself out, it was a matter of a plot moving toward resolution.

*A sermonic idea is a homiletical bind; a sermon is a narrative plot!*

There is more to be said about the nature of a plot, the various kinds and dynamics, etc., but now that we have identified what a generative idea is (at least in a preliminary way), it is time to return to our initial question of how to get started in sermon preparation. My hope is that with this reshaped model, vision, or image of a sermon as a narrative art form, we shall be better able to explore the dynamics of sermon preparation.

# getting started

We can identify two preliminary stages in sermon preparation that typically occur prior to the stage of sermonic formation proper. The first is a state of "wandering thoughtfulness" about the Sunday morning sermon. Likely we have 1) jotted down some notes about possible ideas, 2) read the lectionary passages for the day, 3) pulled out a file containing scattered notes written earlier when planning the year of preaching, and/or 4) checked the denominational calendar. But still we don't know much about next Sunday's sermon. Our task at this point is to gather and sort various possibilities. At best this stage is one of imagination; at worst it is the stage of anxiety.

The second preliminary stage is the stage of decision, when we settle on the idea to be shaped into homiletical form. This stage represents a transition to a very peculiar state of knowing implicitly that a sermon *can now happen*, but not knowing explicitly or precisely *what* the sermon will be. Most of us can identify the successful completion of this second stage as the moment when the question of one's spouse about how things are going can be answered "I think I have one!" More appropriately the response could be "I think one has me!"

After these two preliminary stages have been conquered, we can begin the actual formation of the sermon. But my experience is that these preliminary stages represent the truly difficult portion of sermon preparation. There is an incredible gulf between the "wandering thoughtfulness" stage and the "I have it" stage which is dif-

ficult to bridge. Once done, the rest is downhill! Yet strangely, the
dynamics of that transition from the first to second stage—from
thoughts to sermonic idea—are seldom given the attention they deserve in preaching texts. Instead we are given a geography lesson
on *where* ideas can be found, such as in the Scriptures, the theater,
in pastoral experiences, etc. Sometimes the question becomes a
pretext for a bit of sermonizing about the personal spiritual attri-
butes necessary for preaching. But neither of these deals with the
hard question. The difficult issue is to identify what it is that happens in that transition so easily felt and so hard to articulate.

I recall a conversation I once had with an older colleague in
ministry who was noted for his powerful preaching. I wanted to
know his "secret" and so quizzed him at length. Part of our conversation dealt with precisely the question we are raising here,
namely: How do you move from generalized sermon thoughts to a
genuine sermon idea. I do not remember his precise answer, but I
do recall his difficulty in attempting to answer. The plain fact was
he knew *how* to do it intuitively, but he could not articulate *what* it
was that he did. Most of us face that same problem. Since then I
have asked many pastors what they look for when they attempt the
move from the wandering thoughtfulness stage to the stage of discovering a live sermonic idea. Typically I receive two kinds of answers. First, some will reply: A *theme* or *topic*. Others will reply: A
*problem* or *felt need*. But, alas, like that of my distinguished colleague, their answers do an injustice to their actual abilities.

Both kinds of replies are "correct"—but something is missing.
The first reply concentrates on the substance of the sermon, the
central "message" to be preached. But if this is the central priority
in our sermon preparation we will tend to produce lecture-type
sermons which are strong in content but weak in establishing contact with the congregation. If we follow the advice of the second
kind of reply (focusing on problem or felt need) we likely will estab-
lish quick rapport with the listeners but be weak in content. There
are in fact preachers who fall into these two camps. Paul Scherer
once described them: The one knows what to say but doesn't know
how to say it, and the other knows how to say it but has nothing
to say.[20]

Our prior discussion on the image of the sermon can help identify why Scherer's description is all too apt, and how in the early stages of sermon development we can avoid being included in his critique.

The illustration of the incompleted wall is instructive. Recall that we are taught to see the bricks—not the mortar. Everything (note the word) becomes a "thing"—divisible into parts. Scherer's two kinds of preachers both fall into this trap. One concentrates upon the *answer* as the "bricks" of the sermon. The other sees the *problem* as the "bricks." Both miss the mortar. (Alfred North Whitehead and other process thinkers have done their best to help us not see reality as substance—as bricks—but it is an uphill battle.)

But back to our problem—of moving from generalized sermon thoughts to a genuine generative sermon idea. It seems clear that if we begin the sermonic preparation process by concentrating on the "theme" or "topic" the idea remains static—a lifeless brick. Likewise, a "problem" or "need" is also a *thing*—as dead as a "theme." On the other hand, if a sermon is perceived as a *plot*, formed and shaped by the *interaction* of problem and theme, the sermon idea begins to take on life.

The key, then, to bridging the gulf between Sunday morning thoughts and the generative idea is to think relationally. What I need for a sermon to begin to "happen" is for me to pull my thoughts toward an *intersection point* between need and theme. I mean quite literally that I take my jumble of notes and divide them into two stacks on the desk—the one with problem notes, and the other with theme or answer notes. Then I try to link thoughts from one stack of ideas with the other until a relational gestalt happens.

When a theme of a proposed sermon is thrown against a problem, a sermonic idea may be born. When a problem is pushed against the gospel, the interaction may give birth to a sermon. If, for example, I am considering the possibility of a doctrinal sermon on the Trinity, the preliminary question to be asked is: What problem or bind does the trinitarian formula resolve? Likewise, if I am contemplating a life-situational sermon on fear, the question is: What kerygmatic theme provides the clue for resolution? This process—and our identifying it as such—is particularly important to those preachers who use the lectionary for preaching purposes, and whose sermon work therefore begins with biblical exegesis. It is not enough to probe the question of *what* the text is saying. It is equally important to discover *why* it is saying what it says. The question of *why* is most often the context for the transition into homiletical form.

Every explicit theme presumes an implicit problem; every explicit problem presumes an implicit theme. When this does not hold, there is no sermon! In the tension produced by the interaction of these ingredients, sermons are born. The felt bind between need and theme is central to sermonic form; discovering it is the chief work we do in transforming vague Sunday morning thoughts into a generative sermon idea. This is precisely what my distinguished colleague did week after week (but he didn't know it). And so do we when we do well.

By implication, then, the way to commence sermon preparation is to determine *where* our preliminary thoughts reside—whether they involve a sensed problem or a felt thematic answer. Whichever it is, we must begin looking for its opposite. When they intersect in our mind, a sermon idea is born. One might say that any sermon involves both an "itch" and a "scratch" and sermons are born when at least implicitly in the preacher's mind the problematic *itch* intersects a solutional *scratch*—between the particulars of the human predicament and the particularity of the gospel. It is this intersection point (often *felt* more than known) which produces the sensed certainty that a sermon is in fact about to take shape. (We will explore further these matters in Section Three, after we have considered the shape of the sermon in Section Two.)

Our present discussion also suggests by implication that although we have been taught to conceptualize differing types of sermons by the nature either of their content or context (such as doctrinal, expository, life situational, etc.), it is important to notice that when defined by *form* they are always problem-solutional—whether the context is expository, life-situational or whatever. In his discussion of secular writing, Foster-Harris in *The Basic Patterns of Plot* advises that "just as a good fiction story is always a parable, so a correct fictional plot, the map of the story, must contain a problem, the solution, and the answer."[21] Likewise a sermon in its essential form is a premeditated plot which has as its key ingredient a sensed discrepancy, a homiletical bind.

It is quite possible that the preacher may have begun to think about a sermon at the point of the conclusion—just as a novelist may begin a novel with the final resolution, and fill in the plot backwards. In sermon preparation one begins wherever one is and moves the other way. In presentation the sermon always begins with the itch and moves to the scratch—from the human predicament to the solution born of the gospel.

We might note in passing (we will return for greater detail later) that it is sometimes true that the situation in which a sermon is presented contains the "itch." For example, preachers who follow a Barthian theological model should observe that Barth's pastoral preaching occurred in the midst of a world crisis. The itch was a given. Likewise, sermons preached in light of the Jonestown tragedy had the issue presented by the historical moment.

It should also be noted that "itches" have a lot in common. The Christian estimate of human nature suggests that sin has a common base—and salvation a common source. Both preachers and congregations may be assured that although every sermon needs to be particular rather than general, the proclamation of the gospel is not exclusively tied to one person's capacity for critical analysis of each and every personal and corporate itch. Sermons which deal with the doctrine of the Church also by implication may say something about family life, etc.

Not only is the sense of sermonic tension or discrepancy the clue to the formation of the idea, it is also the key for sustaining the idea through the process of the sermon itself *as preached*. I was taught to "tell them what you're going to tell them, tell them, and then tell them what you told them." Nothing could be more fatal for a sermon! Can you imagine a playwright telling in advance how the story will end, or a novelist revealing "who did it?" in the first few pages? Not unless dramatic tension is introduced in another form. The term *plot* is key both to sermon preparation and to sermon presentation.

# plot forms

Surely there are many options available in defining plot forms. I want to discuss just two quite distinct kinds. The first is the typical movie plot, which begins with a felt discrepancy and moves to an unknown resolution. In the movie *High Noon*, the discrepancy consists essentially in the fact that the town marshal has fallen in love with a woman who is a pacifist. The price of their engagement and marriage is that he will resign his position as marshal, and together they will take up residence in another place and begin a new peaceful existence. The plot thickens, however, with the news that three criminals whom he sent to jail have just been released. They are seeking revenge for what he has done to them and are on the train which will arrive at high noon. The marshal is in a bind. If he continues with his plans to leave town with his bride, he is a coward leaving the village without protection from the vengeance of the desperados. If he stays to face the criminals, he will be faithless to his word to his bride of laying down his guns and beginning a new life. The entire plot is hinged on his dilemma and the painful choice he now must make. The viewers are caught by this basic discrepancy, his bind; their attention is fastened on the ambiguity of the suspense. The play's plot continues to thicken until it moves finally to a resolution unknown in advance.

The second kind of plot is the television series plot which begins with a felt discrepancy (just like the movie plot mentioned above) but which then moves toward a known conclusion (unlike the movie plot). In this second type of plot, the viewers know the star will survive, of course; he is scheduled for next Wednesday at 8:00! But *how* will he survive? That is the key discrepancy. The plot thus involves an unknown middle process. The hero is placed into such an impossible situation that there is absolutely no way he can survive—but of course a way is found, a way which is unknown to the viewers. Several recent television detective shows alter this second type of plot by having the viewers see the crime, know the villain, and know the outcome. The bind has to do with just *how* the detective will be able to find out what we know already. (The television series "Barnaby Jones" and "Columbo" are examples of this type.) In this case the plot is thickened by having the clue to resolution caught by the detective but missed by the viewers, who then are surprised by their denseness and the detective's cleverness.

In whatever type of narrative plot, the event of the story moves from a bind, a felt discrepancy, an itch born of ambiguity, and moves toward the solution, a release from the ambiguous mystery, the scratch that makes it right.

Sermons tend to involve the second kind of plot. The congregation has gathered to worship God. Symbols of all kinds have already made the central affirmation of the incarnation before the sermon begins. The congregation expects the gospel to be proclaimed one way or another, and for Jesus Christ to emerge as Savior and Lord—the answer to the sermonic bind. But how? In what way? For what purpose? This unknown middle ground provides the context for sermonic tension.

It should be noted in the context of the parallel between sermons and literary plots that the suspense of ambiguity—the not knowing what or why or how—is the key to the attention of the audience. In the case of the movie *High Noon*, it is obvious that the viewers are not held by their intrinsic interest in the history of the American frontier, in law enforcement, or in noon trains. Information—correct or incorrect—is certainly learned in the process, but these ideational ingredients, as such, do not shape the form of the narrative. The movement from problem to solution of the discrepancy shapes the form of the narrative. Likewise, it is the homiletical bind being moved from problem to solution, from itch to scratch,

that shapes the form of the sermon, not the biblical, historical, doctrinal, or ethical content. The set of outline notes of our poorer
sermons, however, will likely reveal that they were shaped by the
nature of their substantive content, not by the *process* of the narrative experience that is anticipated. One can easily identify the
"bricks" but the "mortar" is strangely absent. Little wonder we are
tempted to leave our notes and preach it "more naturally."

Note too, that fiction writers inevitably catch their central characters in situations involving *ambiguities*, not contradictories. The
marshal in *High Noon* was being asked to choose *not* between a
*good* and a *bad* but between two goods (or two bads, depending
upon your angle of view). The marshal's problem was in fact that he
had to choose between his *love* for his bride and his *duty* toward his
town. Conversely put, he could be seen either as a *liar* or a *coward*
as a result of his decision. Some choice!

Unfortunately many sermons do not place matters in such life-
like perspective. We are asked homiletically to "choose this day
whom you will serve" (Josh. 24:15)—with the choice being God or
Baal! Frankly, I don't find that a difficult choice! In fact, I have yet
to hear that a parishioner has literally decided on evil as a result of
my sermon!

People are not caught between a generalized good and a generalized bad. They are caught in the bind of two quite specific goods
or two quite specific bads—or (perhaps more likely) among several
options none of which is good or bad. Competent fiction writers
understand the human predicament well. As a result, their fiction
has the feel of fact—of reality, while our fact—our reality—often
has the feel of poor fiction. Often it does not reflect life as people
really live it.

The homiletical plot must catch people in the depths of the aw-
ful discrepancies of their world—social and personal. It is to these
very real discrepancies that the gospel of Jesus Christ is addressed.
Sometimes it appears that perhaps there is no redemptive answer
to the human predicament. This is the bind felt as ambiguity by
people—and this is the discrepancy that is the central question in
every sermon. How can the gospel intersect the specifics of the
human mystery and come out on the other side in resolution? This

question *is* the form of the sermonic plot—which now needs to be seen, first in profile and then in description.

In setting forth a profile of a sermonic plot, I recognize that any generalized pattern is ripe for exception and violation. Yet a generalized pattern is helpful in clarifying the issues and providing the norm from which exceptions are made.

Because a sermon is an *event-in-time*—existing in time, not space—a process and not a collection of parts, it is helpful to think of sequence rather than structure. I propose five basic sequential stages to a typical sermonic process—a plot which may be visualized in the following way:

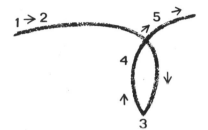

The stages are: 1) upsetting the equilibrium, 2) analyzing the discrepancy, 3) disclosing the clue to resolution, 4) experiencing the gospel, and 5) anticipating the consequences. My students have found it helpful to remember these steps with the following abbreviations: 1) Oops; 2) Ugh; 3) Aha; 4) Whee; and 5) Yeah.

Note that the visualized plot line is forward moving—set horizontally, unlike the outline, which is a vertically imaged static structure. The sermonic plot is time oriented—an event in history with a beginning and an ending. We deal not with parts of a whole but with stages of a sequence. What is necessary now is to explore in greater detail these five stages of a sermonic plot.

# SECTION TWO

## the stages of the homiletical plot

# OOPS !

## upsetting the equilibrium

The first step in the sermon as preached is to upset the equilibrium of the listeners in such a way as to engage them in the sermon
theme. Here we do well to note the approach of playwrights, television writers and novelists. They make the assumption that the
readers and observers are in neutral mentally as the experience
begins. The truth is, different people will be in different forms of
readiness. Some are eager to be engaged, others reluctant. Some
enter the theater after a bad day, others sit down in front of the
television set out of boredom. Some are happy, others sad, etc. All
these matters are taken as moot by the artists who wisely take
full responsibility for eliciting attention/interest/engagement. They
draw us into a world of their own making.

So likewise the congregation gathers on Sunday morning in
many different moods, readiness sets, etc. Too often we who have
been engaged with the theme for several hours, days, or weeks
assume a similar investment on the part of the hearers. Likely, most
listeners know only that a sermon is coming within the context of
worship. Perhaps they have glanced at the title in the bulletin or on
the outside sign. The hopes of some may be limited to the desire
that our sermon won't be too long. It is quite possible that those we

want most to reach with the gospel are those with the least desire to hear.

We therefore need to take major responsibility for their engagement with the theme. What has been our sermonic itch must become theirs—and within a matter of two or three minutes—else their attention will move to other matters. Of course there will be those who will give us rapt attention regardless of what we say or how, but to key on them is to miss our first responsibility.

In the sermon as experienced, upsetting the equilibrium is based not alone on its being a tested literary device; it is born of the nature of being human. Fromm, the psychologist, calls us the "freak of the universe"[1]—the homeless animal. Reinhold Niebuhr speaks of the anxiety consequent of our being both finite and self-transcendent.[2] Ambiguity is thereby felt as foe to be vanquished. The need to resolve ambiguity is theological in nature—that's why it can be used as a literary device. In mild doses it is a motivator both to attention and to action. One cannot breathe easily until some solution occurs. And when resolution comes, the result is both a knowing and a feeling.

So potent is our need to resolve ambiguity—to be at peace—that ambiguity has power even when experienced in pseudo-form. This is one of the reasons children love to hear a nursery rhyme over and over again. Although they know how it will conclude, it is pleasurable to relive the painful suspense of it so that once again the suspense can be removed.

Often in homiletical writings we have been told to "stimulate interest," but are seldom told what interest really is. The consequence is that only *after* a sermon has happened we have a vague notion of whether we did it or not. In my view, interest is the first psychological state of ambiguity. (Advanced states of ambiguity may be fear, dread and repression.) The reason why it is good advice to "talk about people" in sermons is that the introduction of people produces ambiguity—as any storyteller knows. More broadly put, ambiguity exists in any phenomenon which is both vital and at risk. The opening sermonic statement: "Today I want to talk about love" is dull indeed until risk is introduced: "Our problem is that so many times we extend our hand in love only to bring it back bruised and broken. To love is to risk rejection."

John Dewey noted many years ago that thinking begins at the point of a felt problem.[3] Problems are *felt* as ambiguity and hence the introduction of ambiguity is the first step in a sermon as preached. Kurt Lewin, a theorist in change strategy, explains that the process that concludes with change is begun by altering the balance of tension (force field) within an individual or group.[4] Such new imbalance as Lewin suggests (and which we will explore later in greater detail) is in fact what we are calling ambiguity, making it correct to conclude that the primary purpose of sermon introductions is to produce imbalance for the sake of engagement. This comes as no surprise to us if we have observed what happens in the opening scene of a play, the first couple of pages of a novel or the first two or three minutes in a television program. "Conflict," explains Roth, "is the very stuff of which stories are made. So also with life and the world. We are carried on by the suspense. We long to know the outcome."[5]

It should be noted in passing that this is an important purpose to an announced or printed sermon title—to help upset the equilibrium. Most titles tend to do the reverse. They appear to be drawn from the sermon's conclusion (the scratch rather than the itch). As a result, the preacher has to move backward from the announced title in order to arrive at the beginning of the sermon itself. A title known in advance of a sermon should itself be ambiguous—making listeners wonder what the sermon will be about. Once the sermon is presented the title becomes a one-phrase summary of the essential point.

Again, the ambiguity must be felt by the listeners, not just the preacher. It is possible that there may be a small peculiar corner of our esoteric interest in the Church councils of the fourth and fifth centuries which includes ambiguity, but this is not "preachable" until and unless it is translatable to an ambiguity that can be experienced by members of the congregation.

The first step in the presented sermon, then, is to upset the equilibrium of the listeners, and is analogous to the opening scene

of a play or movie in which some kind of conflict or tension is introduced. This opening ambiguity may or may not be related directly
to the major theme of the sermon. The homiletical view expressed
in this writing assumes that ambiguity and its resolution is the basic
form-ingredient to any sermon, whether life-situational, expository,
doctrinal, etc. in content. There is always one major discrepancy,
bind, or problem which is the issue. The central task of any sermon,
therefore, is the resolution of that particular central ambiguity. This
is not to say that the sermon closes down all of life's ambiguities any
more than the closing of a good play presumes to finish the lives of
the central characters. Rather it is that now the anticipated future
is made new by the resolution of one central issue or problem.

The resolution of a central ambiguity also does not mean that
there are no other ambiguities which get resolved in the course of
the presented sermon. Every dramatic or literary plot has numerous smaller subplots that come and go. For example, I recall a
movie in which the opening scene was ambiguous in the fact that
the viewers could not determine what they were viewing. I recall
that I could see a shimmering, wet-like, bumpy surface of some
kind—unidentifiable because the camera was purposely out of focus. As the picture sharpened in focus I could then discern that it
was a rain-soaked cobblestone street I was viewing. By the time I
was able to determine that fact, two feet passed by on the screen—
but whose? As the person walked away from the camera I could
detect the sex and approximate age of the person. The camera followed the person into a building and its elevator. It was not until
the person turned around in the elevator that I was able to see the
face. By that time I certainly wanted to know who the person was
and what destination was in store for both of us once the elevator
opened again. In short, the set of small ambiguities caught me into
the larger and still undefined ambiguity of the main plot—which
soon was to emerge. Likewise a sermon introduction may upset the
equilibrium of members of a congregation by means of an inconse-
quential ambiguity which serves simply to stimulate interest in the
sermonic process. As such it may be as unrelated to the central
discrepancy or thematic problem as was the issue of the unidentifiable rain-soaked street in the movie. Helmut Thielicke often uti-

lizes this kind of introductory/minor ambiguity in beginning his
sermons on the parables. He begins his version of the "Parable of
the Prodigal Son" with these words:

> Several years ago I once set my little son down in front of a
> large mirror. At first he did not recognize himself because
> he was still too young. He quite obviously enjoyed seeing
> the small image that smiled at him from this glass wall. But
> all of a sudden . . . [6]

Note that the illustration of his son has nothing to do with the Prodigal Son narrative. It serves only to whet the appetite of the listeners
who, after hearing the story, will wonder what it has to do with the
biblical story.

One must be careful, however, to determine that what is intended as an opening minor ambiguity for interest's sake does not
occupy the listeners' attention at the expense of the central plot.
For example, I used to begin a sermon on Jonah with the observation in the opening lines of the sermon that certainly it was difficult
for many of us twentieth-century scientifically oriented people
really to hear a story which involved a fish big enough to house a
man whole and carry him around for three days before spewing him
out on the ground safe and sound. With that opening minor ambiguity for interest's sake I moved on to engage the congregation in
the central issue of Jonah's narrowmindedness and the largess of
God's love. Unfortunately, while I moved on, many in the congregation did not. They had not found closure for the minor ambiguity
and stayed with it throughout the sermon. They missed Jonah altogether! One must be reasonably certain that an opening minor
ambiguity is in fact closed. I revised my Jonah sermon by deleting
the entirety of the opening remarks about the story, and started
directly with the narrative itself—which has plenty of ambiguity
already!

(This same problem of minor ambiguities becoming major obsta-
cles to central plot involvement often emerges again with the use
of sermon illustrations. A sermon illustration, for instance, may be
included to concretize a point but have an ambiguity of its own
upon which the congregation's attention becomes fastened—to the
preacher's dismay! I recall a student's sermon which was illustrated

by his own experience of conducting a marriage service. "The father of the bride arrived drunk," he mentioned in passing. He then drew his sermonic point from a portion of the wedding service he had conducted, and moved on to his next point. But what happened to the father? Did he make it through the service? While the preacher made his next point we were still at the wedding—fantasizing what might have happened. I now do not recall what was the next sermonic point. Such is the power of ambiguity and the necessity for closure.)

While the sermon introduction may involve a minor ambiguity not actually related to the central plot, in many cases the initial sentences of a sermon open directly into the central bind or discrepancy. Such was the case in the sermon "A Great Time to Be Alive" by Harry Emerson Fosdick, which began: "This certainly is a ghastly time to be alive. . . ."[7]

As a general rule, when the context of a sermon is the contemporary human situation, whether at the personal or social level, it is likely that the opening ambiguity will be the central or fundamental discrepancy. In the case of expository or doctrinal preaching, it is more likely that the opening ambiguity will serve to engage the congregation in a preliminary bind which in turn opens into the central problem.

In any case, the purpose of the opening stage of the presented sermon is to trigger ambiguity in the listeners' minds. Such an ambiguity is not known simply as an intellectual matter; it is a mental ambiguity which is existentially felt. It becomes a part of their existence at that moment in time, and hence when it is resolved and the gospel proclaimed, the good news is not just something one now knows propositionally, but something one now experiences. More about the experiencing of the gospel later. Now it is enough to understand that ambiguity sets the stage for the sermon to become an event.

Such advice ought to be unnecessary inasmuch as we understand the principle well in the theater, with a novel or in a joke. Suspense in these artistic forms is expected. Likewise suspense is an important underlying fact behind the questionable pleasure we had as children in elementary school when we tripped other children as they walked down the classroom aisles. We knew they could either fall on their faces, or recover their equilibrium. (The one thing they could not do is go back to the last balanced step!) Whatever resolution occurred was a resolution to a felt ambiguity.

Unfortunately, we have been taught to begin our sermons by giving away the plot—even to include in the introduction a one-sentence abstract of sorts. As a result we become homiletical equivalents to a foolish playwright going to center stage prior to the drama to announce the central points to be communicated by the drama. If such were to occur in the theater, the audience, having no further reason to stay, would have sufficient cause to get up and leave the theater. The principle is the same for preaching. The purpose of the beginning process of the sermon is to upset the equilibrium.

The preaching of pastors quite diverse in theological temperament illustrates this purpose of sermonic beginning. For example, J. Wallace Hamilton, in his sermon "Does Christianity Have a Chance?" asks in his opening sentence: "Can Christianity survive in a world where the powerful forces run counter to it?"[8] In "Scandals of Faith" Paul Scherer opens with: "These Gospel lessons, as a rule, seem so neat and simple. And they aren't at all."[9] In the sermon "As a Little Child" Ernest Fremont Tittle begins with these words: "In this saying of Jesus there is something strangely appealing—and strangely disturbing."[10] In preaching on the theme entitled "Did Jesus Distinguish Between Sacred and Secular?" Leslie Weatherhead said: "Wherever I go, I am very concerned to find that the commonest criticism of modern religion is that it seems irrelevant to life."[11] Said Phillips Brooks in the opening line of "The Great Expectation": "It is not easy to decide just what the apostles expected with reference to the second coming of the Lord."[12] And David H. C. Read started his sermon "What Response to Our Prayers?" by asking: "When you pray is there anyone there listening?"[13]

In each of the above illustrations something is left "hanging"—something that needs closure. The fact of incompletion, whatever its nature, is the cause of the listeners' attention. Such disequilibrium on the listeners' part is the key to beginning a sermon. But establishing disequilibrium is only the first step. The second is even

more important—to keep it. Often a pastor will open a sermon with
the binding discrepancy only then to allow it to slip away in the
next sentence or two. For example, the more recent of Gerald Kennedy's preaching typically will raise an important issue only to announce in advance how it will be resolved. In his sermon "God's
Good News," Bishop Kennedy begins with an interesting story of
how Bishop Taylor used to stand on top of a barrel on a San Francisco street and announce to any who would hear that he had "good
news for you this morning."[14] But in a few sentences Kennedy says:

> Tonight I want for a little while therefore to talk to you about
> the Gospel as the "good news," and I want to say three or
> four things. First this: The Gospel is the good news of *per-
> sonality*. It is the good news that at the heart and center of
> the universe there is a person—that God is a person.[15]

You can feel the tension slip away. Suppose he had continued in a
different vein, such as noting that "the bad news for most of us is
the impersonal and dehumanizing state of our experience in the
modern world." After building the tension of longing for the personal, he could finally bring the good news that "at the heart and
center of the universe there is a person—that God is a person."
These words then uttered would answer our felt need and bring
experiential relief. Simply put, answers ought to wait for questions
as felt by the listeners.

One final warning, however, about this stage of a sermon. While
one should not give away the plot resolution, one *must* give direction to the ambiguity. The congregation needs to know the specific
direction of the plot and some of what is involved, but without having the clue to resolution disclosed. Undifferentiated ambiguity
soon becomes no ambiguity at all. The key here is to provide clues
as to the issue at stake and the difficulties of sorting out the ingredients—even the apparent unlikelihood of resolving the matter.
But the lack of resolution at this point is precisely what interest is
all about. The first step in a preached sermon is to upset the equilibrium. Once the equilibrium is upset the sermon then begins the
difficult task of probing the problem.

# analyzing the discrepancy   UGH!

The second stage in the sermonic process *as presented* is the stage of analysis or diagnosis. In most sermons this process is the most lengthy of the five, often requiring as much sermon delivery time as all the other stages combined. In my judgment it is also the most critical stage because the ultimate form of presentation of the gospel is directly dependent upon it. In this stage we must dive directly into the fundamental or central discrepancy, asking: *Why?* Although texts on systematic theology generally deal with doctrines of God and Christ first, and then move on to the question of the human condition, sin, etc., it is my experience that in the practice of ministry, and particularly in our preaching role, the process is reversed. Once a person has revealed his or her position regarding the fall, sin, estrangement, etc., one is able to project with reasonable accuracy the corresponding doctrine of salvation. Those who are fairly optimistic about the human condition, believing for example that sin is some form of ignorance, will (if consistent) emphasize Christ as teacher. Wisdom is the means of salvation. Those who see humankind as hopelessly crippled or entrapped likely will have a "high" Christology to match. The atonement will be the key to salvation. As a practical matter of "doing theology" for most preachers, the cure of the gospel will fit the malady to be solved.

This is consistent with the New Testament record of theologizing. The Gospel of Luke reflects on an ethic of obedience which is predicated on human capacity to respond. In the account of the Last Supper (Luke 22:14–27) drawn from Markan sources the phrase "and to give his life as a ransom for many" (Mark 10:45) is deleted. The theology of Luke/Acts is based on greater optimism than, for example, the writing of Paul, whose understanding of the human plight needs a Redeemer who can "deliver me from this body of death" (Rom. 7:24). So it is that once a person has settled on the question as to what is wrong, the choice of cures is limited. You do not prescribe surgery for a minor cut, nor do you put a Band-Aid on cancer. The question of the human condition is, I believe, the most fundamental and consequential question of all. Surely every preacher is tired of the hackneyed statement—always presented as though never thought before—"Well, I guess you will never be out of a job." Yet, behind that "original" thought is the salient point that our vocation is in fact predicated upon a gap, a void, a discrepancy between what *is* and what *can be* or ought to be. The diagnosis of that gap is central to the task of ministry.

What is true generally in one's theologizing is likewise true in every specific sermon. The particularized problem, discrepancy, or bind provides the problem of every sermon. It constitutes the central ambiguity the sermon seeks to resolve. The analysis of that discrepancy determines the entire shape of the sermon, including the form of the good news proclaimed. Clearly, diagnosis is central to our homiletical task. By analogy everyone who has ever visited a physician with a troublesome malady knows this centrality of diagnosis. A physician without credibility of diagnosis will not be trusted for prescription or prognosis.

Not only is diagnosis—the asking of *why*—central to the content of the gospel preached; it is likewise the chief vehicle for the maintenance of the sermonic plot. Again by analogy, every good detective story "hangs" on the question of "who did it?" and the reader is "hung" by the fact of not knowing—yet—who did it. This ongoing suspense provides the existential *raison d'etre* for continuing to read on. By keeping the *good* half bad and the *bad* half good the contemporary writer avoids the mistake of white-hat/black-hat polarity which allows the reader to get ahead of the writer. For once the "villain" is revealed the story is pretty well over. Likewise the suspense of not yet knowing why things are as they are (given a particular issue) provides the homilist the opportunity of diagnostic wrestling—of theologizing. The congregation's attention is held not because they are enraptured with theology *per se*, but because the bind is not yet solved and there is therefore no option but to stay involved in the sermonic process.

Unfortunately, the greatest single weakness of the average sermon is the weakness of diagnosis. What is lacking is concrete perceptive insight into the multifaceted ambiguities of the human situation which, when revealed, make one reflect: "Of course, why didn't I think of that?" or "Yes, I have always known that without knowing how to say it."

In particular, the difficult yet central task of *diagnosis* is often exchanged for description or illustration—and I believe often without the preacher's being aware of the substitution. For example, to say that "Joe drops cups because he is clumsy" is not analysis—not an answer to the question *why*; it is description. The term "clumsy" is just a more generalized way of referring to dropping cups or other items. To say that Sue was fired from her job because she was "inept" is only to move from the specific behavior of Sue (whatever that was) to the larger context of "ineptitude." We still know nothing about the cause behind the behavior. To say that Frank was unfaithful to his wife because he is a "sinner" is no better; it only abstracts away from concrete behavior to general categories. Rather, what is needed is to move the other direction—from specific behavior to underlying causes.

The medical equivalent to this exchange of diagnosis for description would be the frustrating experience of going to a physician with the complaint of a stomach ache, and upon completion of a physical examination be told you were suffering from "indigestion." "But why?" would be the next question, and a further answer that "you have an inflammation of the digestive tract" would not be satisfactory. As patient you would begin to doubt whether the doctor really knew why it was so, and therefore you would be suspicious about the potential effectiveness of the written prescription. In the book *Tyranny of Words,* Stuart Chase quotes from an actual graduation address once delivered at Colgate College:

> We need a spiritual regeneration, yes, in business as well as other things. It is essential that we achieve a degree of national unity by developing a concrete philosophy for our young men. Those who understand the spiritual background of our country, and understand what our forefathers were trying to do, are likely to be selected for important positions and become successful.[16]

This kind of circular dance among various generalizations is familiar to anyone who has heard very many sermons. What is missing is *depth*—a probing into the causative ingredients responsible for the situation. Diagnosis or analysis is what is needed—not description.

The other often-used exchange for analysis is illustration. Illustrative material can be very helpful in making concrete one's theological analysis—but illustration is not an adequate replacement for analysis. Consider, for example, the issue of apathy. Surely it must be that apathy is a current problem, for I hear sermons on the subject quite regularly. What often occurs is that when the time comes to ask *why* the problem exists, the question is detoured to a homiletical assurance that in fact the issue is endemic to our present culture. At this point in the sermon event we are told about someone in a major city being stabbed while others looked on, then of a low voter turnout in a recent critical election, and finally about the hard time suffered by the nominating committee of the church at the hands of those unwilling to assume leadership roles. Then the listeners are reminded of the value of commitment, self-sacrifice and involvement expected of all Christians. What could have been a proclamation of the gospel turned into a moral exhortation—and one with such a low common denominator that it could have been delivered at the local Kiwanis club by anyone from any religious/ ethical perspective.

Instead of description or illustration, what is needed in this second stage of sermon presentation is depth of analysis. By continuing with the illustration of a potential sermon on apathy, the nature of analysis can be explicated and the nature of the gospel implicated.

I personally have never been confronted with the situation of physical violence and the question of my potential intervention. I have known times, however, when something wrong was happening and I was in the position for possible intervention—and did not so intervene. In those situations I have always known some kind of fear—either of doing the wrong thing, being misunderstood and thereby held in low esteem, or simply of not knowing what ought to be done. I cannot recall any situation in which I was personally involved and failed to respond because I was indifferent. My own personal experience suggests that the problem of apathy always includes other variables which are the cause for the behavior sometimes identified from an exterior vantage point as apathy. Our responsibility in preaching the gospel requires us to probe behind the behavior to motives, fears, and needs in order to ascertain the cause or causes.

Continuing with our example, if the cause of my apathy is fear of rejection, then the gospel will be able to speak to me, because the good news makes it less necessary for me to fear the rejection of others. If my apathy in refusing to accept the responsibilities of a church position is a result of my fear of failure, then the door is opened to the proclamation of the good news that I can be a failure and still be affirmed by God—and therefore am now able to risk failure as I was not before. But if a sermon by use of the term "apathy" simply attacks the fact of my lack of response, likely I will dismiss it either as not applying to me or as not understanding the real reasons for what another has called apathy. Another possible response on my part is to feel guilty that I am such a failure (which in turn will feed my fear and weaken further my capacity to act). Otherwise put, the gospel does not deal directly with apathy at all—but with the varied possible causes behind it. The purpose of the sermonic process of analysis is to uncover the areas of interior motivation where the problem is generated, and hence expose the motivational setting toward which any cure will need to be directed.

Poor sermons are made easy because they remain at the behav-

ioral level, and behavior tends to involve a rather simple either/or
dynamic. Motives, on the other hand, are exceedingly complicated.
Behavioral choice involves an incredible mixture of interior motives. (Sometimes behavior occurs without the involvement of
choice and is then even more complicated.) It is always possible
that a behavioral decision is both complicated and difficult, but because only the decision is visible to the world, it may look decep-
tively unambiguous. For example, the prodigal son decided to
leave home. There were only two options available—stay or leave.
He chose to leave. But behind such apparent simplicity is interior
complexity. Inasmuch as the text does not raise the question of *why*
he left, we are free (somewhat) to imagine, for example, that he had
always disliked his brother *and* always had a desire to see the world.
On balance that was not enough to tip the scales toward departure.
It is possible to speculate further that some significantly negative
encounter with his brother just barely tipped the scales in favor of
leaving—but "barely" is everything in terms of behavior. Either he
stays or leaves; all or nothing at all.

The point of the illustration is that causality is complicated, and
the preacher who does not dirty his homiletical hands with the fact
of the deeper and quite fluid complexity of the motive world will
not be trusted in the sermon, in a counseling chamber, or in the
church board meeting.

For adequate analysis, one must always go behind the "simplicity" of behavior to the complexity of causality. Upon my own personal introspection, I notice how much more merciful I am toward
my behavior than I am toward that of others. The reason is not that
I intend to be unjust—simply that I am more in touch with the
interior complexities of my life than others'. Presuming that I hold
this trait in common with other preachers, I believe it crucial for us
not to cut the world into "we" and "they"—a tendency I find per-
vasive in sermonic work. In particular, it means that when attempting a diagnosis of a particular problem, it is helpful to reflect on our
own personal involvement in the situation. If it is outside our experience, then at least we should consider the problem in the context of those we respect—not of the "enemy." I know of no easier
way to avoid the hard task of analysis or diagnosis than that of deal-

ing with the sins of the enemy. Not only is it true that we dwell in a land of people with unclean lips—we too are people of unclean lips. Hence we will do well to explore the discrepancy within the context of the *we*.

The actual process of diagnosis/analysis in the preparation stage of a sermon is relatively easy to state and difficult to effect. Simply, it is to ask *why* and not be content with your answers. As you continue to reject each answer with another *why* you will find increasing depth in your analysis, until you come across a reason underneath which you cannot go. Often it will have a "feel of peculiarity" about it—as being somehow different or at a strange angle from other answers. More than that, often there comes a revelatory sense of receipt—and you know you "have it." When that moment occurs you will have advanced to stage three in the sermonic plot— the "Aha." Like the lighted light bulb in the old comic strip, its coming signals a decisive and sometimes peculiar form of knowing which illumines the entire plot. As you move along the process of rejecting the initial answers to the question *why*, you will move from the superficial "common sense" answers that are known for their popularity (and from my point of view, their inaccuracy) to the uncommon answer which makes sense in the deepest explanatory way.

This process can best be understood through a couple of extended illustrations. For example: ask just about anyone the question as to why poor folks are poor, and the quick popular "common sense" answer will return "because they don't want to work." Ask again as to why that is so and the typical answer is "because they are lazy." But why are they lazy? "Because they have no motivation." The process continues: "Because they just don't care" . . . "Because they have no self-respect" . . . "Because they somehow lost it" . . . "Because they are failures" . . . "Because they have failed" . . . "Because they have failed at work." By this kind of process it begins to break through that behind the question of *not working* is the issue of *failure at working*—which then can be pressed to a multitude of causes having little to do with the "common sense" variety of understanding motivation. My experience is that the lack of motivation readily observable among the poor is not the *cause* of poverty but its *result*, and that "motivation" in this case—or its lack—is actually an effect of prior causes and deeper motivation. Finally it becomes apparent that when continual failure becomes so painful as to reach the point when it is too damaging to self-respect to continue to try, lack of motivation is the result.

Again the diagnostic/analytical process can be illustrated with the problem of oppression, bigotry, etc.—or simply the event of the "put-down." Why would people want to put down other persons, races, economic groups, etc.? The quickest answer is that "they think too highly of themselves and therefore enjoy looking down on others." It is a matter of arrogance or pride—an illustration, surely, of the garden scene of reaching for the apple. But when this answer is questioned, and one begins to think of *oneself* as the oppressor, it becomes apparent that other ingredients are in the mix. For example, it is possible that pride is a mask that covers the real issue at stake. If so, then putting down people (one way or another) may be a way of feeling better about oneself. Certainly there are many of us who have a rather large need to feel better about ourselves. We may wear the mask of pride, but what is underneath? Continue pressing this issue and (for me) it turns out that people who characteristically put down other people tend to be people who do not like themselves. If this is the case, then self-rejection is the base line underneath the oppressive personality. This conclusion is then the "Aha"—the clue to resolution—which calls for a quite different proclamation of the gospel than does the conclusion that oppressive people suffer essentially from arrogance.

The point of the above two illustrations is not to propagate my particular set of theological conclusions with which many could disagree easily. The point is to clarify the analytical process. Whatever one's general theological position regarding the human condition, that position takes explanatory root, undergoes testing and confirmation, and becomes functional only through the hard task of relating it to specific human situations. Further, whatever the issue, the precision of analysis will determine the correlation of gospel and human condition. When this analysis is superficial, the gospel as proclaimed must of necessity feel like a "pat answer"; it will lack credibility. Ultimately every homilist will have to make some generalized or universal claims regarding the human condition. The shape of these claims will greatly determine the shape of the good news proclaimed. Both Reinhold Niebuhr and Daniel Day Williams, for example, rely on grace to resolve the human dilemma, but because their analyses of the problem are so different, their views on the dynamics of grace are also different—with Niebuhr focusing on forgiveness and Williams upon completion in community.

So far the discussion of the process of analysis/diagnosis has focused primarily upon the preparatory work prior to delivery. One matter related to this process *as preached* needs to be considered. The analytical work of asking *why* should not be completed and then discarded prior to the sermon event itself. Too often preachers have expended considerable energy and perspiration on an issue, resolved the diagnostic question to their satisfaction and then brought their conclusions to the pulpit. But the process of analysis not only provides the occasion for the content of the preached Word to happen, but also the ambiguity necessary to sustain the listeners' attention. It is clear, therefore, that the *process* of analysis as well as the *conclusions* from analysis need to be shared with the congregation. By analogy, most people evidence only slight interest in a given piece of furniture, but considerable interest in the making of a piece of furniture. The reason for this is that a completed piece of furniture involves closure; it is done. But a piece of furniture in the making involves ambiguity. Interest—as has been mentioned—is a function of ambiguity.

Hence, the preacher should go through the process of analysis *with* the congregation—surely less involved and more ordered than happened in the study—but nonetheless in a fairly complete way. The question of *why* should be asked again in the pulpit, even though the matter has already been resolved for the preacher. Otherwise the end result of sound analysis may be received as authoritarian instead of authoritative. It is the same principle as the process involved in the detective story. The reader is constantly asking: "Who did it?", making preliminary judgments and then revising them along the way. Of course the author already knows who did it—but the issue is for the reader to undergo the drama of discovery. In fact, a good detective story writer will "help us" make numerous wrong conclusions along the way, only to set us on other possibilities. When the author finally reveals the villain, the revelation of it is experienced by the reader with a sense of both pleasurable foolishness and considerable relief: "Of course it was he; why didn't I know it sooner?" Likewise the sermonic process of analysis *as presented* moves the listeners through numerous dead-end routes until the decisive clue is disclosed. By commencing with superficial "common sense" answers to the question of why people behave as they do, and then continuing to press the analysis ever more deeply, the preacher engages the congregation at the level of popularly held views which then may be abandoned together in favor of more thoughtful analysis until at last the decisive clue to resolution is revealed. For the clue to resolution (stage three) to be existentially real, and for the gospel to be experienced (stage four), the context must be prepared by the ambiguity explicit in the analysis of the discrepancy. The purpose, then, for stage two is not simply for a resolution to be reached but also for a *readiness for resolution* to be developed.

These various issues we have considered in this section on *Analyzing the Discrepancy*, such as 1) moving from superficial analysis to in-depth diagnosis, 2) building listener readiness for resolution—even by the inclusion of analytical "dead-ends," and 3) hence setting the stage for the Word to be proclaimed, are all manifest in the preaching of Helmut Thielicke, one of this century's great homilists. His sermon "The Parable of the Pharisee and the Publican" captures our attention in the first two opening sentences:

> This parable is so simple and seems to have about it so much of the quality of being beautifully self-evident possessed by things with which we have been familiar from our youth that we hesitate to waste another word upon it. Why should we as adults dissect and analyze and mull over what a child understands?[17]

"But" he notes immediately, "often we miss the inner mysteries of the very things with which we are most familiar. . . ."[18] Thielicke perceives and notes in the first two minutes of the sermon that the parable runs the risk of having "a point so self-evident as to be downright banal."[19] The reason is that the modern reader has become cynical about Pharisees and sentimental about publicans. Thielicke deepens the ambiguity and heightens the interest by re-*image*-ing both Pharisee and publican—noting that the Pharisee was as good as he claimed and the publican as bad as he admitted. Once he accomplishes this, the listener is by now confused as to why the publican could go home justified but not the Pharisee. Thielicke goes toward further "confusion" by noting the similarities of the two men: both standing before God in thanksgiving, etc. By this time the listeners are inwardly crying out for some resolution to the question *why* (in this case not why the two men were as they were, but why Jesus was the way he was). At long last Thielicke arrives at the clue to resolution and says: "this is where we hit upon the salient point."[20]

Throughout the entire process, Thielicke moved from the initial upsetting of the equilibrium to the analyzing of the discrepancy—ever increasing the felt tension of ambiguity. Finally, with the readiness for resolution keenly developed, he was ready to announce the resolution he and the listeners would be prepared to accept. He then moved on to *Disclosing the Clue to Resolution*—and so shall we!

# AHA!
# disclosing the clue to resolution

The overarching purpose of the process of analysis (step two) is finally to arrive at an explanatory *why*, first for the preacher in the study and then for the congregation in the sermonic event itself.

All problem-solving processes, whether scientific endeavors, literary plots, medical diagnoses, dime-store puzzles, or preaching on Sunday morning, look for some missing link, some explanation which accounts for the problematic issue. All share the assumption that we live in a cause-effect world—that nothing happens for no reason. When found, the missing link is the bridge from problem to solution, from itch to scratch. Stage two of the sermon presentation process moves with increasingly felt "necessity" toward some kind of release, toward the revealing of the missing link. Once disclosed, matters are seen in a different light. (This decisive turning-point is reflected visually in the plot line diagram above.)

It is also typical of the problem-solving process in whatever endeavor (scientific, medical, etc.) that numerous "dead-end" answers are discovered and discarded. We have already discussed (in stage two) how the preacher often experiences a number of such dead-end answers—those which seem at first to explain *why*, but which on further examination do not. These "false conclusions" are analagous to one's experience with a detective story in which the reader becomes frustrated in pinning the blame on the wrong suspects. Against such an analytical wall, often there comes a resolution, a clue which feels revelatory. In it one senses the missing key which "unlocks" the whole. Until found, the matter seems irresolute; after being found, the matter seems self-evident! In gestalt terms, it is the "aha," the one piece which allows the whole puzzle to come into sharp focus. Such a revelatory clue is *experienced* by the congregation rather than simply *known*.

Moreover, there is a peculiarity of the homiletical "aha" which I call the *principle of reversal*. It is often the case that the clue making understandable the issue at stake comes as a surprise. It is not quite what one had expected, and "arrives" from where you were not looking. And *it turns things upside down*. In the visualized plot line shown, the radical change of direction is intended to suggest how the sermonic idea is turned inescapably by the clue; things can never again be seen in the same old way. More concretely, there is in fact a reversal which takes place—the term is not a figure of speech. Foster-Harris, in describing "the physiology of fiction" asserts that "the answer to any possible problem or question you could pose is always in some fantastic manner the diametric reversal of the question."[21]

Before taking a look at several homiletical examples of the principle of reversal, we will explore our experience with reversal in other fields, such as literature, humor, television stories and puzzles. By doing so we will better understand the theological/homiletical application.

The principle of reversal appears in classic form in Plato's famous allegory of the cave. The prisoners are chained together in such a way that they can see only a back wall of the cave. A fire behind them and moving figures make flickering shadows on the wall. They believe the shadows are reality. If released to see the fire and the figures their perception of reality would be utterly reversed. But suppose, said Plato, that the prisoners are led out of the cave into the sunlit brightness of noonday. Wouldn't they be struck dumb by the impossibility of it? Such a radical reversal into reality might in fact drive them back into the cave.

Truth, Plato is saying, is a radical reversal. Hence, so is the form of
the story.

Likewise, reversal happens in Shakespeare's *King Lear*, not
once but successively. Frederick Buechner describes the result:
"Foolish old Gloucester has his eyes put out but then suddenly, for
the first time, sees the truth about himself and his sons. Mad old
Lear loses his crown and his kingdom but at the last becomes for
the first time truly a king."[22] Then the last act brings the tragic ca-
tastrophe and reverses the reverses again!

Reversals occur quickly in the typical joke:

> Sir Oliver was an elderly member of a prestigious hunt club
> in England. Whenever the members gathered for tea, they
> would turn to a senior member of the club to relate an un-
> usual personal experience in the sport of hunting. It was Sir
> Oliver's turn. "Well," he said in a quavering voice, "one time
> we were hunting elephants in Africa. We had spent the
> whole day tracking an obviously large bull—and had just
> about given up hope.
>
> "All of a sudden as we came to the top of a hill we looked
> down and there in the clearing, there he stood—the largest
> bull elephant I have ever seen. Gentlemen, I raised my gun,
> got the bull in my sights, and . . . and just as I was about to
> pull the trigger, I heard a rustling in the bushes off to my
> right. I glanced over, and just a few feet away . . . there was
> a bengal tiger! And . . . (Sir Oliver raised his arms) . . . And
> he went: ROARRRRRRR!
>
> "And . . . and . . . I'm ashamed to admit it to you, but
> gentlemen, I . . . I . . . I wet my pants!"
>
> —to which a younger member of the club replied: "But
> Sir Oliver, you shouldn't be ashamed of that. It could hap-
> pen to anyone at that kind of moment."
>
> "Not *then* you fool," replied Sir Oliver, "Not then . . .
> just *now* . . . when I went: ROARRRRRRR!"[23]

That is a reversal of figure and ground. The figure is the hunt,
the ground the story as told. The humor arises as a form of shock at
being jolted by the punch line's reversal of that figure and that
ground. "Quickie jokes" do the same: "Were you a drop out?" "No,
I was born Caesarean!"

Although not every joke form contains as radical a reversal as
the above two, nonetheless, the humor is occasioned by the sudden

shift which is unexpected. We know the sudden shift will come, of course, but we do not know when or how.

This sudden reversal in preaching comes as the clue to resolution reverses the train of diagnostic thought. The resultant shock does not come in the form of humor, but in the form of release by means of sudden illumination of the homiletical puzzle. No wonder Craddock in *As One Without Authority* complains that to preach deductively (starting with the generalized resolution first) is like starting a joke with the punch line![24]

The movie *High Noon* referred to in Section One contains the reversal event which occasioned neither humor nor release by means of sudden illumination, but rather the relief from the pain of ambiguity in the "impossible" possibility of reaching a happy conclusion to the plot. Actually there are two reversals necessary in the story. You will recall that in the movie the marshal leaves town with his bride—preferring honor to duty—to start a new peaceful existence. But the farther the couple travels, the more the marshal becomes aware that his pacifist bride, although happy about his decision, would in fact never be able to respect him—having left the town defenseless. He decides to *reverse* direction, go back to town and face the returning criminals for the inevitable shootout. By the time he gets to town, however, it is already high noon; the desperados have arrived and with weapons drawn are making their way to the marshal's office. As a "coincidental" result of his being late, he gains the advantage of being able to surprise them from behind. By the time his gunfire has killed two of the men, however, his reversed approach is no longer a surprise to the third gunman. In horror, we perceive that the gunman has the draw on the marshal; we see the outlaw's gun raised in aim; we hear the gunfire and are surprised to see the outlaw fall to the ground. The camera turns and we view the pacifist bride holding the decisive weapon.

In the case of *High Noon* the marshal could not possibly have won the battle against the outlaws without the author taking him out of town first in order to provide the advantage by reversal. Even then, with three against one, the marshal's advantage slips away—only to be regained by the reversal of the pacifist bride. Now we surmised all along that it would somehow turn out right—but the writer lured us into dead-ends (such as his leaving town, and then upon returning facing three-to-one odds) in order to provide the context for the surprise of happy resolution. It should be observed also that one means of enhancing the setting for the reversal event is to escalate the situation by means of detail. This occurs in *High Noon* by the vehicle of having the town's shop owners turn into cowards and board up the windows of their businesses—just when the marshal is about to decide to leave with his bride. The reversal in the movie *The Sting* is a matter of the viewers being placed in the privileged position of being "in-the-know" regarding the various characters' experience of being conned—only to be catapulted into becoming the principal victim of the game at the last moment.

It would be unreasonable to assume that Sunday after Sunday, the ordinary preacher is going to provide such dramatic, jolting, or funny reversals as I have just illustrated from plays and jokes. Nonetheless, the principle has validity and can be accomplished much more easily than one might think. The two illustrations utilized in the previous section on analysis both contain significant reversals which are crucial in the diagnostic turn toward the "Aha." A return to those illustrations of homiletical analysis should prove helpful at this point.

The first illustration dealt with the analysis of why poor folks are poor. The reversal involved is that in asking the question *why*, people generally concentrate on the situation of someone not looking for work, whereas (from my point of view) the key has to do with the situation when in fact they *were* working, and failing. For that reason I noted that "my experience is that the lack of motivation readily observable among the poor is not the *cause* of poverty but its *result*." Now, that statement is a statement of reversal which radically changes one's view—literally turns that matter upside down. It shifts from the view that "people are poor because they are lazy" to the conviction that "people are lazy because they are poor."

The other illustration used in the section on analysis dealt with the question of the oppressive personality, and moved from the view that the reason why people put down other people is that they "suffer essentially from arrogance" to the view that "self-rejection is

the base line underneath the oppressive personality." The concep-
tualization of *self-rejection* as the key is a direct reversal from that
of *arrogance*.

Regarding these two illustrations on poverty and oppression:
the first involved a cause-effect reversal and the second an inverted
cause reversal. Another kind of reversal, the reversal of assumption, is used extensively in puzzles (at our expense!).

In the figure below are nine dots which become a puzzle when
we are asked to draw four straight contiguous lines which will go
through all nine dots (or one continuous line in four directions).

Typically we are caught with one dot untouched—no matter where
we start or how we move:

Our problem, you see, is that we made an assumption, namely that
the dots constitute a box. We think we are supposed to stay within
the space "enclosed" by the dots. Now this assumption is not part
of the instructions at all. We simply presumed it to be so—an unconscious "rule" we brought to the problem. So we are at a loss to
work the puzzle successfully.

Now, let us reverse our assumption. The *clue to resolution*, the
*aha*, is that instead of assuming we have to "stay inside" the box,
the truth is that it is necessary to go *outside* the lines. Once we
make the reversed assumption the puzzle is solvable in a matter of
seconds:

The critical issue of this puzzle for our purposes is to note the radical difference of approach *once the clue was given.* Once known, solution is just a matter of time. The clue served to reverse the underlying assumption. Before the critical clue is given the matter seems irresolute; after successful completion it all seems so self-evident. Such puzzle experiences are examples of the principle of reversal utilized in literary plots, jokes, and sermons.

The peculiar talent of the puzzlemaker (a rather sadistic one at that) is that talent of "helping" us to make the wrong assumption. Once made, the puzzle-solver is held in bondage. Likely, the more obsessed (interested) we are with a puzzle, the more active is the conviction of the wrong assumption—and hence the greater the bondage. Except by good luck, only by *consciously questioning* our assumptions can we begin the process of extrication and resolution. The "principle" behind this puzzle is common also to most dime-store puzzles—namely that "common sense" inevitably will keep the victim on the wrong track. Resolution comes only by reversing the assumption of "common sense."

The intrinsic power of the rut called "common sense" explains (in reverse fashion) the experience of serendipity. The reason that flashes of insight come when one is not looking is that our cognitive ruts lose their tenacious hold upon us when our mind is occupied with other things or begins to drift as we go to sleep. Hence, the unthinkable thought (generally inverted from common sense) has a chance to break through. Such uncommon sense comes as an intuitive "aha."

Unfortunately, the more we know about a subject, the more apt we are to stay locked into our assumptions, and hence to become blind to alternative perspectives. So believes William Gordon, who is convinced that experts in all fields are particularly vulnerable to the counter-productive power of "common sense." In his book *Synectics*[25] he explains his method for developing creative solutions in the business world. Because the "experts" seem trapped by mental blinders, Gordon's method uses small groups of persons unfamiliar with the technology or discipline in which the problem has occurred. Being "innocent" of experienced perspective, these novices are often able to provide solutions the experts cannot discern because of their expert common sense.

So too, the expertise of the homilist may produce blinders preventing resolution of an issue. In many cases crucial diagnostic resolution will come only by reversing the particular assumption—just as was true in the case of the puzzle. How this mental process works in the homiletical context is explained best by example.

I once heard a sermon on the theme "Finding Yourself" which was preached in a fairly large Protestant church in a university city in the midwest. It was delivered in late May or early June—about the time for graduation. No doubt the minister had envisioned the situation of high school and college graduates who are experiencing a critical moment of life-transition—either from one academic situation to another or from the academic setting into the "wider world." The theme of self-discovery would be particularly appropriate for those people—and not inappropriate for others as well.

The sermon began by upsetting the listeners' equilibrium by noting that many of us "have difficulty knowing who we are." Explaining the cruciality of self-discovery, the minister began asking *why* the problem was so persistent. Before resolving that issue, however, and moving to some clue to resolution, the question of *why* was replaced—inadvertently, I think—with the question of *how*. "How can we find ourselves and know our identity?" After noting such false means as "trying to become rich or famous, etc." the pastor moved to the scriptural text: "But to all who received him, who believed in his name, he gave power to become children of God" (John 1:12).

This he said is the "clue to finding one's identity," to solving the quest for self-discovery. He explained the meaning of the text: "Once a person begins to identify with God's will as expressed in Jesus, and begins to behave accordingly, that person will experience self-discovery." Now, there is some truth in this logic to be sure, but the sermon struck me as flat and without surprise.

In spite of its "good sense," the sermon's heavy dosage of the ethic of obedience bothered me theologically, and more importantly, omitted some deeper truth of the gospel. I began the process of mental evaluation of the sermon and recalled that he never followed through the process of analysis. In particular, he seemed to be operating on the basis of some diagnostic assumption not stated in the sermon itself—and perhaps not even consciously known.

I began to explore the issue of this particular sermon and discovered an assumption analogous to the one involved in the puzzle. His assumption seemed to be that a sense of personal identity is continuous with and should be the ultimate result of one's search for self. Presuming my evaluation to be accurate, the question is: Is this so? Is it true that those who seem "in touch" with themselves witness to a prior deliberate self-discovery process? Or conversely, do those who have engaged in a self-discovery process typically report having "found" themselves?

My answer to both forms of the question is no. I have known numerous persons who have been "looking for themselves" for a lifetime without success. And many there are whose sense of identity never involved any kind of conscious search for self at all. In reflecting on my own life, I observed that those times when I have seemed most in touch with myself, when my self-identity has been most secure, have been those times when I was *known by another*—not by myself—*and was accepted by that other*. I then recalled someone's having said that "those who give their lives in search of happiness will find many things, but never happiness." Could it be that the issue of self-discovery is analogous? I believe it is. My assumption now is that one's search for self ultimately is fruitless because it seeks to *find* that which can only be given by another. In short, we may seek self-identity and hope to find ourselves, but the hoped-for result never occurs through our own efforts. *We seek ourselves, but are finally found!* One's identity is the gift of another's love.

Returning to the sermon as preached, the pastor apparently was operating on an assumption—unstated and perhaps unconscious. It was this assumption which kept the sermon flat and without surprise. The surprising clue to resolution, the "aha," the reversal could have emerged at the end of the analysis stage by noting the futility of self-discovery—"ask the wrong question; get the wrong answer!" That twist could have turned the sermon upside down and opened the door for the proclamation of the good news of Jesus

Christ—that in fact *we have been found* by a love incarnate that will not let us go.

Without this reversal of assumption the only option left, homiletically, is for the preacher to urge us toward greater efforts to find ourselves and to do God's will. Good advice, perhaps, but hardly the good news! Says Foster-Harris, in reference to secular writing: "The method of solution invariably is to invert, to reverse, to 'twist' the problem picture so that a new picture abruptly emerges."[26]

Although this present focus on assumptive reversals is set within the context of the decisive homiletical turn of analysis, the same principle is effective throughout the sermonic process. Helmut Thielicke's sermons provide many illustrations of this kind of assumptive turn. For example, in his sermon on the Prodigal Son, "The Waiting Father," he notes the possible assumption of motive regarding the son's experience in the pig pen and his subsequent repentance. Thielicke asserts that it is not true that having run out of his luck and having hit bottom, the son's motive is purely self-serving. Says Thielicke: "It was not because the far country made him sick that he turned back home. It was rather that the consciousness of home disgusted him with the far country."[27] Or again, Paul Scherer's intuitive feel for the power of reversal is evidenced constantly in his writing and preaching—sometimes including double reversals. Once he noted that "we sing 'God Bless America,' and it never seems to occur to us that he may find it very difficult. What is worse, it never seems to occur to us that if he succeeds we may not like it!"[28] The assumptive reversal can be discovered in Fred Craddock's writing as well. In pursuing a train of thought regarding biblical preaching he observed: "It is not only more blessed to give than to receive; it is also much easier."[29]

The process of reversal as presented in a sermon can be likened to the action of pulling the rug out from under someone. Often it is necessary to *lay* the rug before one pulls! This is particularly true in biblical narrative sermons, and especially in the parables of Jesus. Because we are so familiar with the parables, it is difficult for us to grasp how often Jesus "laid the rug" before he pulled it out. For instance, we know that the Samaritan is the hero of the story named for him before we begin it. Our image of the term "Samari-

tan" already has been formed by our familiarity with this parable.
Hence, there is little surprise when we re-tell the story and arrive
at the expected moment when the Samaritan bends down to aid the
victim of attack. Not so with the listeners of Jesus who held the
Samaritans in lowest esteem. Those listeners would know intuitively that what looked like helpful behavior would turn sour. It
would have to because he was, after all, a Samaritan. Surprise! As
I suggested in an earlier section, we miss the point of the Pharisee
and the publican story because we falsely assume that the Pharisee
is a phony and the publican not all that bad.

Because these stories are so well-known it is imperative for the
preacher first to cultivate the assumption Jesus knew would be held
by his listeners, and which he then intended to rip away. For instance, we all know the elder son is the "fall guy" in the story of two
sons. So, unfortunately, it comes as no surprise when we label him
appropriately for refusing to join the celebration. But Jesus told the
story to a fairly "righteous" crowd who could readily identify with
the elder son's anger at such an injustice as that. They knew the
difference between the faithful Hebrew who was obedient to the
covenant, and the unrighteous one who had turned traitor to his
heritage and unfaithful to his God. This was the context for Jesus'
preaching on the Kingdom as recorded in Luke. To end the story
with the unrighteous inside the party and the faithful outside the
door was surely a scandalous way of depicting God's ways with humankind! Believing the same mentality to be active in our time,
Craddock asks: "Are you *really* in favor of parties for prodigals?"[30]

If we are to be true to the parable in our preaching today, some
means must be devised for re-establishing the context—or at least
preparing the listeners for the shocking end of an otherwise lovely
story of repentance. Not only is that means available by utilization
of the principle of reversal, but the text itself gives the clue to the
decisively illuminating turn. In our re-telling of the story the elder
son should be portrayed in his faithfulness. The listeners should be
encouraged to identify with his anger. After all, who hasn't had the
experience of being faithful and loyal only to have the party given
for someone else. It is in fact quite upsetting for hard work to be
rewarded only by more hard work while irresponsibility is re-

warded with festive homecomings. (Remember, too, that the elder son was coming in from overtime work in the fields which caused him to be late for dinner!) Who hasn't known the time when the award, honor, or promotion went *not* to the one whose faithful presence went unnoticed because in fact he/she was always in proper place, but rather to the one noticed for his/her unpredictable presence? Make no mistake about it—the party was unjust!

There will be few in any congregation who cannot resonate with that complaint and the deep interior hurt it represents. Hence it is imperative for the congregation to make that identification. But then, with the "rug well laid," it is reversal time. If the elder son's case is so solid, how does it happen that Jesus' story leaves him outside the reunion? The clue to resolution is given by Jesus in his description of the elder son coming in from the field as the party was commencing. If we did not know the story so well we should think that portion of the narrative quite peculiar. The natural expected behavior of a son coming in from the fields, and who sees, hears, and smells the unexpected at the house would be to quicken his pace and go in with some degree of excitement. But Jesus has him draw back, summon a servant over to him in order to inquire what his father is up to! The portrait given by Jesus is one of a suspicious son, who in fact does not trust his father (contrary to our previous assumption). The music and dancing were surely clues to him that it was a happy surprise—except (apparently) that what might be happy for his father likely would not be the same for him. Note that this spontaneous and revealing reaction on his part takes place *before* he receives word of his brother's return. Hence, the rest is rationalization. The reader now knows that no one can trust the elder son's pious protests about justice. With this sermonic reversal the elder brother's character is revealed and the parable clearly identified as a story about a father and his two lost sons.

This story is not peculiar among the parables of Jesus in the inclusion of remarkable surprise. Things seem never to turn out as expected by the listeners. I believe it fair to characterize the parables of Jesus as noteworthy (among other reasons) in the fact of their inclusion of reversal.

Moreover, this feature is not unique to the parables of Jesus; it can be found throughout the Scriptures. The story of Abraham's sacrifice of Isaac includes a reversal in that the command to sacrifice his son involved an interior contradiction. The issue involved is not simply that Abraham was commanded to make the ultimate sacrifice any father could make. The point is that Isaac was the *only* means to the fulfillment of God's promise to Abraham. To ask Abraham in the name of the covenant to destroy the only means of fulfilling the covenant is logical nonsense. It is a reversal to logical thought which often is called paradox, and finds its ultimate articulation in the words of Jesus: "For whoever would save his life will lose it; and whoever loses his life for my sake and the gospel's will save it" (Mark 8:35). Surely his statement is a summation of the ultimate reversal of the faith!

My colleague, Dr. Lindsey Pherigo, has suggested that the Apostle Paul, too, employed the principle of reversal. In the first two chapters of Romans, Paul seems to be speaking contrary to the theological position commonly ascribed to him. He appears to be advocating an ethic of obedience—with the claim that God "will render to every man according to his works" (Rom. 2:6). What seems to be his clear word, however, turns out to be the preliminary (and inverted) word drawn from the law. After noting that given this point of view, there can be no advantage to the Jew, Paul "pulls the rug" by affirming that "since all have sinned and fall short of the glory of God, they are justified by his grace as a gift" (Rom. 3:23–24a). Moreover, boasting now becomes excluded "for we hold that a man is justified by faith apart from works of law" (Rom. 3:28). In short, the first two chapters of Romans reflect the dead-end avenues of thought which must yield ultimately to the reversal of grace over law.

What is being alleged here is not that Paul, Jesus, or the writer of the Abraham story necessarily intended to utilize the principle of reversal, obviously; it is that there seems to be a common thread of narrative plot procedure which in fact constitutes what can be labeled the principle of reversal. A survey of contemporary preaching could (or should) reveal the same phenomenon—however intuitively or intentionally accomplished.

Moreover, the principle of reversal which occasions the homi-

letical "aha" is more than just a literary device or good strategy—
although it is that. I believe it has its roots in the gospel itself. To
claim that the preached Word is a "stumbling block to Jews and folly
to Gentiles" (I Cor. 1:23) surely is to suggest that there is something
about the gospel which is upside down to the world's way of viewing
truth. Otherwise the "foolishness of God" would not be "wiser than
men," and the "weakness of God" could not be "stronger than men"
(I Cor. 1:25).

There is a *radical discontinuity* between the gospel and worldly
wisdom which itself constitutes the underlying reversal. It seems to
be almost axiomatic that the Lord of history has a long record of
pronouncing a firm NO to the world's *yes* and a resounding YES to
the world's *no*. The essential point of the new hermeneutic school
of thought is in fact to turn biblical interpretation upside down in
order to conform to the truth of the *gospel* as *inversion*. Craddock
actually used the term "radical reversal" in summarizing that point
of view, and explains that:

> One does not begin with the idea that we have in the New
> Testament verbal statements that are obscure into which we
> must introduce the light of understanding; rather, one lis-
> tens to the Word hopeful that it will shed light on our own
> situation which is obscure. The Word of God is not inter-
> preted; it interprets.[31]

Nowhere is the sense of inversion articulated more clearly than in
Barth's section "The Strange New World Within the Bible" found in
*The Word of God and the Word of Man.*[32]

The fundamental mistake of the liberal Protestant pulpit of the
last forty years is that it presumes that the gospel is continuous with
human experience. It would be closer to the truth to say that the
gospel is continuous with human experience after the gospel has
turned human experience upside down. Barth notes that we come
to the Bible with our questions, and find only our own reflection,
instead of "a new world, the world of God."[33]

The trouble with the "neo-orthodox" reaction to liberalism,
however, is that in the process of being true to the gospel, the position becomes untrue to human experience—especially in the
preaching event itself. The liberal preacher is apt to make effective

contact with the congregation and its human needs, fears, and hopes, but to effect little or no homiletical transformation. The Barthian preacher, on the other hand, is apt to walk into the pulpit with scriptural exegesis and exposition as the initial homiletical approach, only to discover that when the time comes for application the congregation has long since walked out existentially and left him there—standing on his head with the gospel! To recall Paul Scherer's sentiments: There are two kinds of preachers. The one has something to say but doesn't know how to say it, and the other knows how to say it but has nothing to say. I nominate the Barthian for the former case and the twentieth century liberal for the latter.

Is there a way of avoiding the two untenable positions identified by Scherer? I believe the view of preaching as a narrative plot which includes the principle of reversal as the decisive clue to resolution offers another alternative. The preached sermon as I am envisioning it begins with the establishment of contact with the congregation at the point of their human predicament and moves through stage two (analysis) inductively in good liberal tradition form. But rather than mobilize the resources of the gospel to fulfill human aspirations, it reveals such human aspirations for the dead-ends they are. By disclosing the clue to resolution, which typically involves some kind of reversal, it opens a new door, and prepares the context in which the Word of God can be proclaimed—deductively ordered in good Barthian fashion.

Central to this schema, then, is the principle of reversal—which may occur in at least four forms: 1) the cause-effect reversal, 2) the inverted cause reversal, 3) the inverted assumption reversal, and 4) the inverted logic reversal. Once the clue to resolution is articulated, the hearer is ready to receive the Word—to discover how the gospel of Jesus Christ intersects the human predicament.

# WHEE !

# experiencing the gospel

Once the clue to resolution has been disclosed, the problematic context is ripe for the experiencing of the gospel. As in medicine, diagnosis is the tough critical process. Once a physician is reasonably sure that matters have been probed underneath the symptomatic level to the causative base, it is a relatively simple matter both to predict prognosis and prescribe treatment that corresponds to the condition. Patients who insist on immediate treatment without proper diagnosis are a pain to the good physician and often discover that the treatment of their condition does not solve the problem.

In the more crucial context of our ultimate concern and the corresponding gospel, it is likewise true that people are impatient for answers and the homilist eager to "get on with it" and tell the folks what the gospel says about the matter. Typically this attitude results in circumventing or detouring proper diagnosis *and* also in losing the ambiguity necessary for listener interest. I call it the *homiletical short circuit*. What often happens is that the sermon plot takes a giant and ill-fated leap from the beginning of stage two (analysis) to stage five—which is the stage of anticipating what can be or ought to be done in light of the intersection of problem and proclamation of the gospel.

Returning to our consideration of the question of poverty, the question of *why* (stage two) is avoided by such a homiletical short circuit, and folks are reminded (stage five) that "God helps those who help themselves." If the analysis of this issue as articulated in a prior section is correct, such admonition surely is to help poor folks become poorer. If, in the previously used illustration of the oppressive personality, the matter is not diagnosed, the superficial conclusion of pride probably will be concluded with the exhortation that we should not think too highly of ourselves "because all have sinned and fall short of the glory of God" (Romans 3:23). Again, if our prior analysis is correct that the real cause is self-rejection, the exhortation will serve only to make matters worse.

On the other hand if the problem of the oppressive personality, when pressed to the causative base line, is that of self-rejection, then quickly it becomes clear that the gospel's answer to self-rejection is a new kind of self-affirmation born of God's unfailing love toward us. The good news is not that we *should* stop rejecting ourselves, but rather than we *no longer have to* reject ourselves because we no longer need to justify our existence. Likewise, the search for one's identity (to cite another previously used illustration) is doomed to failure because it rests on the false premise that it is incumbent upon us to be successful in the search for self. Instead, the gospel declares that we have been found—that identity is a gift one can never obtain or reach on the basis of human effort. In all these illustrations note how clearly and concretely the Word can be heard once the clue has made ready the context!

But note also how important sermonic timing is to the matter. In the last illustration it would be fatal homiletically to announce this good news at the beginning of the sermon. The congregation must experience aesthetically the utter futility of the search before the good news is addressed to the matter and releases the sense of futility. Timing based on the creation of proper context is the key. As a matter of fact, the gospel as preached is a relatively uncomplicated matter. Whether it is credible or not is dependent upon the context in which it is set.

Let us imagine for sake of illustration that I am in another state lecturing on preaching to a group of pastors—no doubt in the basement of First Church. The telephone rings in the church kitchen and the attention of my listeners is diverted momentarily (because the ring of the telephone has more ambiguity than my lecture). Someone calls me to the phone. At the other end of the line is my wife who says: "I just called to tell you I love you." I have a hunch that at such a moment I might suggest to her the inappropriate timing of the otherwise kind message, and remind her that she could have waited until evening and called me at my motel room.

Now, let us change the context of this imaginary call by presuming that my wife and I had engaged in a quite hostile exchange just prior to my departure from home, making our relationship somewhat problematic. Now in this context the telephone rings in that out-of-state city; I am called to answer it and my wife says: "I just called to tell you I love you." The difference of impact can be sensed immediately. The words are identical. It is the context that is different—and the significance is transformed. In one context the words are kindly but inappropriate; in the other way they are reconciling and redemptive.

This is precisely the case in any sermon. Stages one, two and three are intended to prepare the way so that when the gospel is then proclaimed it is *effect-ive*—that is, it *does* what it says, and *is* that to which it refers. As Donald G. Miller puts it: "To preach the gospel, then, is not merely to say words but to effect a deed."[34] When that experience occurs by means of the sermon, we are able to grasp the biblical understanding of the term *proclamation*, which includes both the act of proclaiming and the content of the proclamation itself *in one event*. It is, as P. T. Forsyth asserts: "The Gospel prolonging and declaring itself."[35]

Once again it should be noted that the actual content of the proclamation of the good news must be consistent with the diagnosis which precedes it. The illustrations I have given here, of course, reflect my own particular understanding of the human condition. But the principle is valid whatever one's theology. The cure must always match the disease. As I view the matter, sin most often is a distorted good and I therefore hunt for the good which lies underneath the evil. The gospel calls evil by its proper name, but it also understands the sinner. Our task is to bring judgment on the evil and still love the sinner.

It is commonplace in contemporary fiction to reveal the bad side of the *good* and the good side of the *bad* in order to maintain the ambiguity of mystery. I happen to believe that the matter holds for fiction principally because it is fact rather than fiction. We are in truth complicated creatures whose goodness is never pure and whose evil is never complete. Hence to look for bad motive in good behavior and to seek noble intention in an evil situation is not just to be effective artists in our work, but to be true to the gospel's estimate of human life. But whatever your particular theological convictions and leanings, the good news of the gospel as you understand it will be unavoidably clear once the clue to resolution has been found and matters are turned around in anticipation of the answer.

As a result, our preaching difficulties lie not so much in stage four—experiencing the gospel—but rather in stages two and three. If the diagnostic process of stages two and three results in the clue to resolution, the matter will be illumined and the hearing context prepared for the receipt of the gospel of Jesus Christ. Seldom in preparing for a sermon formed according to this process have I had difficulty in discerning what the gospel had to say about the issue at hand. On those infrequent occasions when I have had difficulty, I discovered that my problem was not with the gospel or in my understanding of it; the problem was that I had not probed deeply enough in diagnosis. When I have done my diagnostic homework and the decisive clue has emerged, the good news has fallen into place sermonically as though pulled by a magnet.

Once again we should note the theological view regarding "point of contact" implicit in this image of the sermon as narrative. It is a view different both from the inductive process of the liberal tradition (which views the gospel as continuous with human experience) and from the deductive process of the neo-orthodox tradition (which views the gospel as discontinuous with human experience).

For example, my view is in sharp contrast with that of Harry

Emerson Fosdick who spoke of "the garnered wisdom of the ages"[36]
which can help meet the problems of human existence. (Note the
sense of continuity between problem and answer.) Likewise my
view is in equally sharp contrast to Paul Scherer, who opposes the
inductive method,[37] admonishing the homilist not to meet the listener "where he is" because "too often he is in the wrong place."[38]
(Note the sense of discontinuity between problem and answer.) The
third alternative as expressed here is to view the gospel as continuous with human experience *after* human experience has been
turned upside down. Hence I begin inductively (with Fosdick),
move toward the clue to resolution which reveals the dead-ends of
the "human fulfillment" mentality and turns matters upside down,
and then proclaim the gospel deductively (with Scherer). (The visualized plot line reflects this fundamental inversion.)

The significance for us at this point in the homiletical plot description is to note that with the hearing context now prepared by
inversion, the experiencing of the word can occur as *event*. "As the
Word came in the flesh," notes Craddock, "so the Word comes in
the form of human speech."[39] It will not be difficult at this point in
the plot process to discern its coming.

With the gospel proclaimed, the homilist is then ready to ask:
What consequences can now be anticipated as a result of this intersection of gospel and human predicament?

# YEAH !

# anticipating the consequences

By this time in the sermon *as preached* the discrepancy has been analyzed, the clue to resolution revealed and the good news experienced. The tension of ambiguity in the homiletical plot is beginning to be released. The critical matter left for explication has to do with the future—now made new by the gospel. Plot-wise, it is the stage of effecting closure. The transition line of Paul writing to the Romans reveals this move to futuristic expectation: "What then shall we say to this?" He then begins to explicate matters now made new by the gospel by asking rhetorically: "If God is for us, who is against us?" (Rom. 8:31). In like fashion the preacher asks: What—in light of this intersection of human condition with the gospel—can be expected, should be done, or is now possible?

This transition to future expectation is common in literary plots of all kinds. It can be seen in the simplest form in television series. For example, Marshal Dillon and Kitty in the television series "Gunsmoke" always had a drink together in the saloon to enable the viewers to anticipate the future. Perry Mason always had a visit with his secretary or client. In the television classic "Roots," the release into future expectation came when the road sign signaled their arrival into Tennessee. It continued with their looking over their new land, and was completed with the brief conversation with Alex Haley himself showing pictures of the succeeding generations.

It should be noted that in "Roots," the writer kept the tension prior to this phase as long as possible. The whites had been tied to the tree and warned not to interfere again, the wagons were gathered in a line ready to set out, and Tildy began to reminisce. The viewers held their breath hoping she would not reminisce too long lest they be caught before their escape to freedom.

In the sermonic plot, the clue to resolution does not "solve" the issue; it only makes solution now possible. The good news is proclaimed, thus facilitating what Luther identified as that "acoustical affair" called faith. In the light of the revelatory moment of intersection both preacher and congregation consider what difference has been made for us. Whatever the issue, this final phase of sermonic closure will suggest a new door opened, the new possibility occasioned by the gospel—which is, as Paul Tillich's title identifies it, *The New Being*. The old has passed away; "Behold, I make all things new" (Rev. 21:5).

A comparison with the more traditional type of sermon construction will be helpful in becoming aware of the difference here. I was taught to begin the sermon with an announcement of the issue together with a brief statement of the solution. The body of the sermon consisted of an elaboration of that solution which generally involved an intertwining of scriptural passage and contemporary situation. All these processes were to lead to the high point of the sermonic "asking"—which constituted the conclusion. One was to have everything lead toward that "call to commitment." This final call or claim was the *climax* of the sermon—its big moment. As Ilion T. Jones advised: "the last point should be the major climax to the sermon."[40]

A sermon seen as narrative plot appears similar but in fact is quite different. Its apparent similarity is in the fact that the final stage of "anticipating the consequences" is in the same relative position, time-wise, in presentation as the climaxing "call to commitment." But there are two important differences. First, unlike the traditional sermon, the crucial moment in the sermon as homiletical bind is not in the "asking" but in the resolution stage when matters are turned upside down, and thereby seen in a new way. The mounting tension—as in any plot—begins to break at stage three (about three quarters of the way through the preached sermon). Resolution occurs at stage four when the gospel intersects the newly seen situation, and the "asking"—the anticipation of the consequences—is then a further view of the differences now made possible by our responding to the gospel. The parallel to this difference—which is more easily experienced than explained—can be noted in the theater. For instance, Arthur Miller's play *Death of a Salesman* does not move to a climax at the end of the play, but shortly before—at the point of Willy Loman's suicide. His death resolves the suspense of the plot, but is not the play's conclusion. Most literary plots find their climax in the moment of resolution sometime before the ending. It is the resolution which releases the tension, and then a brief time is spent in setting matters in place as a result of that resolution. This "setting matters in place" is the equivalent to the sermonic "asking." It anticipates how life can now be lived.

The second difference is more explicitly theological. Although many would deny wanting such a result, making the "climax" of the sermon coincidental with the "asking" of human response constitutes a form of works righteousness, no matter how much the preacher tries to avoid it. It is internal to that approach. The focus of our preaching is upon the decisive activity of God, not upon us, and hence the climax of any sermon must be stage four—the experiencing of the gospel. Human response is subsequent to that experience—and consequent of it. The covenant is initiated on the other side; our part is responsive—and even our response is a divine gift. To make the "call to commitment" the central focus of a sermon is to place ourselves in the limelight, where we have no business being. The "evangelistic" bumper sticker slogan "I found it" reveals this theological error. One does not "find it" at all. One gets found! To be sure, having been found makes possible a whole new set of options, choices, and decisions which need sermonic articulation. But these choices do not make matters whole—the gospel does. Otherwise put, freedom is not an interior human capacity which needs but a homiletical push from time to time in

order to function. *Freedom is a consequence of the grace of God.*
Human freedom is therefore not a reservoir of capacity the
preacher seeks to shape into a "decision for Christ" by means of the
sermon. Human freedom is the capacity for choice that is *generated*
by the gospel of Jesus Christ as proclaimed.

Kurt Lewin, secular theorist in behavioral change, writing in
*The Planning of Change*,[41] notes that there are two basic means of
initiating change in a person or group. Believing that any static state
is a balance of tensions on either side of the status quo:

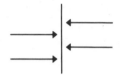

Lewin says that change can be achieved by two means: first to in-
crease tension (pressure) "behind" the static state in the direction of
the desired change:

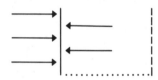

or second: to diminish tension (pressure) which exists between the
static state and the desired change:

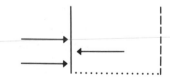

Given these two options (and a possible third—a combination of the
two) Lewin warns about the push from behind: "In the first case,
the process . . . would be accompanied by a state of relatively high
tension . . . [which could result] in higher aggressiveness, higher
emotionality, and lower constructiveness."[42] The danger is that once

the change agent is absent, things are apt to recoil back to a position worse than the first. Many pastors have had the unfortunate experience of following a "push-type" pastor, who was always increasing pressure on a congregation toward his/her own objectives. Once gone from the parish, that pastor does not have to face the judgment of a worsened situation—but the succeeding pastor inherits it.

I recall my experience of having to attend sales meetings when I was a Fuller Brush dealer during my college days. Those meetings always involved an "inspirational" push. We would receive our monthly kick from the back side, and be told to remember that "your sales will reflect directly and exclusively the number of doorbells rung." He was never in touch with the fact that my problem was not lack of motivation, but shyness of personality which resulted in the fear of doorbells. Had he understood this fact and helped remove my fear (and hence reduce the tension) I could have increased my profit—and his. But he did not understand and therefore continued his push from the back side (which was quite ineffective once I was out in the field alone). Hence I continued to perform at a level beneath my "potential."

Frequently I have remembered that experience when called upon to "spearhead" some program by delivering an "inspirational address" at a "kick-off banquet." The image is powerfully clear. I was being asked to push people—at the very least to engage in a "will-nudger" which was supposed to prime the pump of their good intentions.

But is it not true that most people are doing about as well as they are able? Never once in over twenty years of preaching have I been confronted with people who had "decided" to do less than they felt they could. I believe it is unlikely that the trouble lies in a lack of will to intend well. Sermons which assume the problem to be lack of will invariably boot from the back side. But I do believe that people are hindered from doing and being by many other factors. The oppressive personality (discussed earlier) which is engaged constantly in putting people down is behaving out of necessity—not freedom. (Some of us *need* others to look down upon so that then we can bear looking at ourselves.) The redeeming focus

for change is not to browbeat such people by reminders of the resultant evil. The redeeming focus for change is to remove the
necessity so that they no longer need to look down upon others.
This is precisely what the gospel of Jesus Christ provides. It is a
release from evil necessity into the freedom of loving others as we
love ourselves. And we can now love ourselves because in fact we
are loved by God. No longer *having* to prove our own worth, we
may now be set free from making others prove themselves to us.

I am claiming here that the gospel is not a push from the back
side of our lives into goodness but a release from the inevitability
of doing evil. The proclamation of the gospel must be other than a
weekly "guilt trip" placed on our parishioners. The awfulness of
human guilt needs redemption, not a lecture. The preached Word
makes possible the redemption into new life by its announcement
of what God has done and is doing. Sermonically, this means that
the central issue is the proclamation of that good news. After it is
experienced, then the sermon may address the question of "What
then shall we say to this?" In the above illustration, the anticipation
of the consequences could be varied. The "call" born of this new
freedom in Christ may be addressed to the oppressive personality—
indicating that such people now no longer need to look down on
others. It may be a call to the congregation to invite more oppressive people into the congregation in order to experience such release from bondage. It may be a call to love unlovely people. It may
be a call to political action. Whatever it is, it is predicated on a *new
situation* being created by the gospel—a new freedom to make
choices we could never before make. This last phase of the sermon
articulates the possible consequences which now—thanks be to
God—can be anticipated.

With the above description of the closure stage of the sermon as
preached, the entirety of the sermon-as-narrative process has been
considered. Although I have tried to anticipate and address the
various kinds of questions which arise typically with this preaching
rationale, no doubt there are many more which could be addressed.
There are three such questions in particular which deserve our attention here. The first has to do with the question of variety. Should
we invariably follow the five stage sequence? If not, when, and

how? The second question (or group of questions) has to do with sermon preparation. Although I have addressed these several questions in a preliminary way, now that the entire process is before us, it is time to look again at the process of preparation. Finally, the question of biblical narrative preaching, often cited in these pages for illustrative purpose, needs to be explored again, with the inclusion of several pointers which I hope will prove helpful in this particular form of the homiletical plot.

To these three kinds of considerations the third section is focused.

# SECTION THREE
## other considerations

# variations

If the narrative plot line as explained is to be seen as normative for the preaching event, then what about the issue of variety? Would not the invariable following of this approach lead to the same dullness as the traditional three point message? In one sense the answer is *no*, because the traditional three point sermon organized by the logic of content and viewed, as Craddock puts it, "as a rational discourse rather than as a community event"[1] is already ripe for boredom. Yet it is certainly true that any method utilized Sunday after Sunday in precisely the same fashion will wear thin—particularly when the process structure is clearly visible. As Craddock observes, "Usually, for the skeleton to be showing, with a sermon as with a person, is a sign of malformation or malnutrition."[2]

On the other hand, there is one essential in form which I believe indispensable to the sermon event, and that one essential is ambiguity. Ambiguity is the glue that holds listeners and ideational movement together. Let us therefore consider how ambiguity can be preserved while variation of form can be facilitated.

I have observed, for example, that I do not utilize the five step process when preaching a biblical narrative sermon. The reason is clear: the biblical narrative already has its own plot, and hence its own ambiguity to be settled. It does not need another plot line superimposed on top of it. In truth, the purpose of a narrative plot form is to make any sermon—life situational, doctrinal or expository—a narrative event. A parable of Jesus does not need the reformation because it already is a narrative event. More broadly, any sermonic presentation of a narrative of any kind, biblical or otherwise, should be allowed to run its own narrative course. The principle of reversal, nonetheless, still holds true and generally can be found within the narrative itself.

Variations within the five steps are also possible. Craddock notes, for example, the need to have something for the listeners to do as participants in the sermon—and warns against providing too much closure. He hopes that as a result

> [the] congregation cannot shake off the finished sermon by shaking the minister's hand. The sermon, not finished yet, lingers beyond the benediction, with conclusions to be reached, decisions made, actions taken, and brothers sought while gifts lie waiting at the altar.[3]

What this means specifically in the five step process is to leave unstated or only hinted what might be the anticipation of the consequences to the narrative plot. This ending before articulated closure is increasingly being used in movie plots. Sometimes to the point of agitation for the viewer, the end of a contemporary movie is more problematic than its beginning. This "cool" style (à la McLuhan) may be more effective—or at least more tolerable—for a younger generation raised wth television.

Likewise it is true that the opening stage of the sermon (upsetting the equilbrium) in fact may be unnecessary. As I mentioned in the treatment of that stage of the presented sermon, it is wise for the homilist to assume responsibility for listeners' interest as they may bring little readiness into the preaching experience. This, however, is not always the case. Funeral sermons, for example, do not need any vehicle to upset the equilibrium of the listeners. The fact of death—often visible by the presense of a casket—has already upset the equilibrium. The preacher does not need to take time and energy to do what death has already done. The same is true whenever an event in the congregation or in the world in fact has upset the equilibrium. Recall the Sunday after the assassination of President Kennedy. Because of the trauma of that tragedy and the incredible need for closure in understanding, it was difficult *not* to preach powerfully. (It may well be that the fact that Karl Barth's

world was already upside down accounts for his not attending to the
need for upsetting the equilibrium of listeners in preaching.)

In the mid-fifties several hundred tourists were caught and ma-
rooned by a flash flood in the Pocono Mountains of eastern Penn-
sylvania. Many persons close by had died in the flood and destroyed
roads kept many of us from leaving the area. That Sunday the village pastor addressed the congregation on the subject "The Will of
God." Needless to say, we hung on his words! (Unfortunately, his
failure to provide closure did not have the powerful effect that lack
of closure in contemporary films produces.)

It is likewise true that there are numerous occasions when long,
involved diagnostic processes are inappropriate. The trauma of grief
involved in the loss of a loved one, for instance, makes intensive
cognitive participation virtually impossible. To ask someone to do
so is a form of cruelty. Likewise, a liturgy of a festive celebration in
the life of a congregation is no time for lengthy exploration of causality of some discrepancy. On the occasion of an important congregational anniversary, for example, a former pastor's sermon may be
"held" sufficiently by the ambiguity of past memories and their rec-
ollection.

Then, too, there come those extraordinary moments in the life
of the church when a pastor faithful to the gospel and to conscience
must bring a prophetic, healing, troubled, or celebrative witness to
the congregation which by its very nature violates any and all sermonic rules. Such moments make their own claim and abide by
their own rules. Generally, the context is a supercharged one which
provides so great an ambiguity that it becomes unnecessary to
worry oneself with cultivation. Sometimes an occasion will preclude
several of the normative stages of a sermon—even the explicit proclamation of the gospel. As such, these times involve a presentation
not properly called a sermon at all—and yet justified. Any pastor
will recognize these occasions for witness for what they are, and
should not be troubled greatly that they become exceptions to the
normative principles of preaching. If, on the other hand, a pastor
discovers that these "special occasions" are becoming less special
and more routine, then it is time for the evaluation of possible
causes.

But the more likely means of achieving variety in sermonic form while maintaining necessary ambiguity of plot is in altering the form of the discrepancy itself—from the question of *why* something is true to another kind of discrepant question. In Section One I noted that there are several kinds of plots experienced in drama. I expressed my view that generally the sermonic plot is similar to the television series plot in which the end of the episode is known, but unknown is *how* the process will arrive at the known conclusion. The Columbo television series varies that theme in having the viewers know everything except how Columbo is going to figure it out. Likewise, sermonically, the question of *why* a situation is as it is may be known; the discrepant issue therefore may be *how* a congregation can intercede in that situation. In the explanation of Section Two, I illustrated the narrative plot line with the discrepancy being *why*, but it could also be the issue *how* or *when* or *where*. Likewise, it is possible for a sermon more nearly to resemble the movie plot line in which the outcome itself is unknown. Prophetic sermons often need this kind of ambiguity in order to avoid defensiveness—as surely Nathan knew when he asked David what he would do in the case of a sheep stealer. In the mid-sixties, I heard a sermon preached relative to the oppression of the native American in previous generations. We in the congregation thought the ambiguity had to do with the situation at that previous time. We were all justly indignant at what our forefathers had done, and were engaged in wondering what the right prophetic voice might have said to alter that reality. But the homilist turned things around at the last minute to say that the sermon was not about the white man's oppression of the Indian then; the sermon had to do with white people's oppression of blacks today. It was too late to become defensive!

Often dialogue sermons in which more than one person is preaching involve the type of ambiguity illustrated by the typical movie plot. In a dialogue sermon the ambiguity consists in the congregation's not knowing how the differing points of view will be resolved. Many congregations have experimented with dialogue sermons and have been disappointed at the results. The various kinds of failures are generally related to the issue of discrepancy or ambiguity. In the case of a congregation's being surprised at a traditional sermon's being "interrupted," the surprise factor only works once—and even then the congregation's attention often is diverted from the issue at hand to the question as to how well the participants are "acting out their roles." Conversely, many dialogue sermons suffer from the lack of ambiguity. The two participants may have rehearsed their dialogue sermon to the point that all significant differences evaporated prior to Sunday morning. On the other hand, a dialogue sermon which becomes polarized into two extreme positions on a subject becomes a win/lose debate and listeners' attention is diverted from the ambiguity of content to the felt necessity of choosing sides. The problematic nature of dialogue sermons helps identify the cruciality of ambiguity in any sermon, and serves notice that sermons may fail in communicating the gospel not only because of the lack of ambiguity and the boredom which ensues, but also may fail by too much ambiguity which blows the circuits of comprehension.

Whatever kinds of variation are utilized in the plot formation of a sermon, the glue of appropriate ambiguity is necessary. People do not listen for *no* reason—and any "reason" *is* some form of discrepant bind which clamors for resolution.

# preparation

Having explored the plot of the sermon as preached, it is time to go back to the question of sermon preparation. Where does one begin, and how?

I noted in Section One that a sermonic idea may be born from various sources—a passage of Scripture, congregational needs, an ethical issue, etc.—and that the sermonic idea emerges at the intersection point between problem and solution, between the particularities of the human predicament and the particularity of the gospel, between *itch* and *scratch*. Further, I suggested that our first task in sermon preparation, then, is to identify *which* of these two poles is in fact our beginning point and move in thought in the opposite direction until the discrepancy or bind is known and felt. This is *what* we do to begin, but *how* precisely? The best way to find out is to select a text and try it. Paul's confession in Romans 7:24 will suffice: "Wretched man that I am! Who will deliver me from this body of death?"

The first thing to notice is that it is obviously a *problem* (itch) text. With that observation, we know that if a sermon is to be born, the issue of Paul's sense of bondage from doing the good must therefore be pressed toward some solution (scratch) born of the gospel. But note that to do so at this level of generality will probably fail to yield the generative idea that has felt discrepancy. If left in this form, we might likely move to another Pauline text for the solution: "I can do all things in him who strengthens me" (Phil.

4:13). But such quick resolution does not give birth to the bind. The two texts simply stand in juxtaposition to one another with a felt sense of contradiction. What is needed is to make the problematic text more concrete, specific, or limited in scope. This we do by asking ourselves questions about the issue.

*In what sense* does Paul need to be delivered from his body of death? Is it a problem of will, ignorance, or what? Secondly, is it true that his problem is ours also? Can the issue once identified be translatable to the contemporary human scene? It is likely that only after some such diagnostic work is accomplished will the text be ready to be moved toward the solution. This is the reason I noted earlier that the intersection point is felt more intuitively than conceptually and more implicitly than explicitly. One may sense that he or she "has it" in terms of a potential sermon—but only after more analytic work can "it" be brought to articularity. In the case of the two texts in this illustration, the sense of discrepant bind may be felt simply by noting that both are taken from the same person. How could Paul the Christian utter both statements? Unless one statement assumes a pre-Christian context while the other text assumes a Christian context, or the former question is rhetorical, or one of the two texts is in fact not Pauline (or unless he is talking out of both sides of his mouth) then we have a problematic bind. Is there some peculiar way in which any Christian could make both statements at once? Clearly it is time to engage in serious biblical exegesis. At this point in our consideration it is unclear to me what the results homiletically might be (having not preached on this text in some time), but I *do* sense intuitively that a sermon is in its embryonic stage; I feel the bind. And I cannot help but sense that it would likely relate to my own personal experience. Upon continued reflection, I note that what started out to be two texts—one *problematic* and one *solutional*—has turned into two texts that are problematic by their relationship, made discrepant by the fact of their contradiction.

Another text chosen for a possible sermon may be a *solution* text—in which case we would note that fact and begin working from the other direction. In this latter instance we must begin to move toward the problem implicit in the solution. Typically solution texts are even more general or global than problem texts, and must be pressed into specificity before one can move to the problem.

Sometimes a preacher is surprised by a text which fits neither problem nor solution context and is in fact the decisive clue to resolution. Standing midway between the two poles of human predicament and solution born of the gospel, the text reveals—at least by implication—the whole. Almost every pastor upon occasion has had the unusual and joyful experience of sitting down to begin work on a sermon and having the sermon unfold almost immediately—and with the amplified notes completed in a matter of minutes. It is f42quite likely that such an experience was occasioned by the discovery of a text or other material that was in fact the clue to resolution. The reason the preparation task in such a situation can be accomplished so quickly is that everything was revealed at once. Such moments are rare indeed.

In any case, the preparation process begins with the identification of whatever material or thoughts one has—that is, whether problematic, solutional or resolutional. Immediately the preacher presses the matter into more specificity and begins to consider the opposite of things in order to arrive at that intersection point where the discrepancy or bind is known and felt. When the tension of the bind is known, the sermonic idea is born. The material is set within the sermonic plot pattern in order to discover what other preparatory work needs to be addressed. Almost always the most difficult part of the task of preparation is to engage in the process of diagnosis or analysis of the basic discrepancy. When the clue to resolution is found, it should make existentially credible the prescription of the gospel and the sermonic articulation of the subsequent consequences which may be anticipated.

Because the principle of reversal *per se* is new to most homilists, and because it is so critical in the diagnostic stage of the sermon, some discussion of how to prompt its discovery is in order. If it is true that we tend to be blinded by conventional wisdom, and we happen not to be lucky enough to experience serendipitous moments, what can we do? Are we not left in a rather helpless position—analogous to the person told to be "spontaneous now"? Not quite.

Often when I am in the process of analyzing the discrepancy and no reversal reveals itself, I try to "help it" happen by the following means. On a piece of paper I list every conceivable reason *why* a situation is as it is. I will have perhaps a half-dozen to a dozen "reasonable" but not illuminating diagnostic answers to the problem at hand. I then go through the list asking these and similar questions of each written answer: Could it be the opposite of this reason? Could this be the effect instead of the cause? What alterable assumption lies hidden behind this answer? By asking these questions the clue, the reversal, generally appears.

Wherever in the plot line one begins preparation for a sermon, all the sermonic material born of scriptural reference, human experience and the homilist's own thought processes must be placed ultimately within the process framework of the sermon as preached. Once again, it is imperative that the preacher not discard the struggle of the study and simply report the results in the pulpit. Not only are people unimpressed with and disinterested in others' conclusions *per se*, it is an insult to their personhood not to be involved in the process itself. As Craddock notes:

> It bears repeating that a preaching event is a sharing in the Word, a trip not just a destination, an arriving at a point for drawing conclusions and not handing over of a conclusion. It is unnatural and unsatisfying to be in a place to which you have not traveled.[4]

But perhaps the most important issue regarding the preparation of a sermon has to do not with the specific process itself, but with the kind of preparation that should happen before one sits down to begin any sermon. My best sermons began when I was not looking for one. There is a kind of sermonic drought that is apt to set in upon me whenever I am intentionally working on a sermon. Sometimes the harder I try the further away the potential sermon seems to flee. And there is good reason for this phenomenon—one already introduced in these pages in a different context.

Recalling the discussion of the difference between conventional wisdom and the surprise of the gospel, and remembering the principle of reversal, we can understand the dynamics of such sermonic drought and also of the serendipitous experience of having a sermon happen when you are not looking. In the discussion of "disclosing the clue to resolution" the issue of serendipity was mentioned in passing. The context at that point was the bondage of conventional wisdom at work in a specific sermonic issue. The point now is that this same bondage is at work *immediately prior* to sermon preparation as well as *within*. We are all creatures of the cultural wisdom which infests our culture not only while wrestling with an issue, but even as we "hunt" for a sermonic idea. Its ubiquitous power resides principally in the fact that it works beneath the scenes of our conscious thought. Out of this context we perform our homiletical work. Even when knowing full well that a surprise twist is going to be in order, and that somehow the gospel will turn everything upside down, yet our blinders are on working well. As I mentioned earlier, conventional wisdom has us, and the harder we concentrate, the greater the power of the blinders. This power is particularly strong at that moment when we know we must begin work on a sermon but do not have any potential idea in mind. So we turn to the Scriptures and begin to hunt. The more we search the less we find. At this moment it seems that necessity has become the mother of a total mental blank.

But when studying the Scripture for its own worth and our own sake (or in reading other material) the blinders of conventional thinking are not so strongly on guard. For this reason—in addition to other quite sufficient ones—it is imperative that every preacher engage systematically in a self-directed reading program which not only can help one become a better informed professional but which can provide the setting for such serendipitous revelation.

Likewise I have learned (thanks to my colleague Dr. Charles Baughman) that our study of the Scriptures will be more productive homiletically when we utilize several translations immediately (as well as Greek and Hebrew texts). Too often we will hit upon a stimulating text and turn quickly to the exegetes to receive their findings. The consequence is that our homiletical vision is narrowed quickly at precisely the time when it should be broadened. As a result we become locked in not only to our blinders but also the blinders of the "experts."

I have found one other technique to be particularly helpful in avoiding my own mental blinders in the reading of the Scripture. Foster-Harris in the work already cited notes the importance of viewpoint in the process of creative writing. By this he means that every story is to be created from one character's point of view.

> Everything is told with direct reference to him, and nothing he cannot see, hear, think, or feel can properly be included in the story.[5]

Hence this character "actually is conceived and written in the first person, even though the formal third person may be used,"[6] whereas "other characters in the story are drawn in real third person."[7] As a result the reader is kept to the perspective chosen by the writer. There seems to be no problem in this fact until one considers the impact of it when reading a passage of Scripture one has read dozens of times and heard as the text for numerous sermons. What happens in this situation is that such perspective often becomes blinding. The ruts of past experience keep us locked in. Moreover—and particularly when reading passages from the four Gospels—our natural piety keeps us identifying with the perspective of Jesus, God and righteousness. (Our listeners "enjoy" the same tendency.) Breaking out of conventionality in this context can occur readily if one chooses another perspective. New insights can occur, for instance, when one asks how the "woman taken in adultery" scene would feel if you were one of the men gathered in the circle—rather than from the perspective of Jesus or the woman. This technique was the one I utilized in preparing the sermon on the Prodigal Son narrative referred to earlier in this writing. I asked simply: How would it feel to be the elder brother coming in from the field?

These suggestions of techniques for breaking out of the ruts of conventionality—and all other suggestions of techniques—need finally to be set in proper context. All matters of technique have to do, not with the desire to be clever, but rather with the intention to be alive and open to the surprise of the gospel. If we expect our hearers to be changed by the Word, and if we presume that preaching may occasion such change, then we need to be ready for change ourselves. There is no way we can produce the change, but we do have the responsibility of doing those things which will place us in optimum position so that we may be changed by the power of the gospel. Sermonic preparation, then, is not simply the occasion for our "creative work" but for the work of God. We are but "midwives" in the kerygmatic moment. Sermonic preparation is difficult principally because of this "provisional character of preaching"[8] as Barth puts it. Hence, the role of the homilist excludes the producing of the end result. But let us be faithful in performing the task which is ours—namely to set the stage. And that means setting the stage for ourselves first before presuming to set it for anyone else.

# biblical narrative preaching

The task of forming a biblical narrative sermon is much simpler than that of forming other kinds of sermons, such as topical, life situational, doctrinal, expository, etc. The reason is that these other kinds require translation into narrative form—the theme has to be turned into story in order to become an event-in-time. (Most of what we have been about in this book has centered on this translation to homiletical plot.)

A biblical narrative already is in plot form and hence needs no such radical transformation. It has its own ambiguity to be resolved. Rather than *our* going on a narrative trip with a topic, somebody else already has, "once upon a time."

This does not mean that all Scripture passages are to be considered narrative. The term *narrative* itself means a description of events, real or fictional. Hence the ingredient of *time* is necessary for the term "narrative" to be utilized. This means that Paul's description of love in I Corinthians is not a narrative; his description in Galatians of his Damascus road experience is—and hence requires less re*form*ation for the pulpit.

There is a significant trend toward biblical narrative preaching at the present time—at least in the homiletical circles with which I am familiar. Many see this trend as a result of the revolution of mass media. Certainly anyone who has read the work of Marshall McLuhan would expect such to be the case. Some attribute it to the move toward "theology as autobiography"—as illustrated by the writing of Sam Keen and Harvey Cox. Others see in it a move to greater biblical authority. It may be a case of topical preaching growing thin and tired. Whatever the causes, I welcome the trend.

Many homilists, however, believe they are not the "story telling kind" and thus are afraid to attempt this type of preaching. The assumption is that a few preachers have the "gift" of story telling; the rest of us do not. I believe this *not* to be the case. Certainly it is true that some preachers have an intuitive grasp of the principles of story telling. It is likewise true that those who do "have the knack" seem *not* to be able to tell others how to do it. But this does not mean it is an unteachable/unlearnable art. More likely it means that we have not isolated the variables of learnable skills necessary to become good story tellers. And, as is the case of so many kinds of capacities, the matter may be more an *un*learning task than a development of new skills. The average child is a far better story teller than the average adult. Something has happened to most of us through formal education and the culturally induced and regulated perimeters of defined "maturity." Most pastors who have attended seminars I have conducted at Saint Paul School of Theology are surprised at how well they can tell a familiar biblical story if they are instructed to "paraphrase and elaborate it in your own words."

At the same time there are several considerations in the art of story telling which are useful to mention—both for the sake of biblical narrative preaching *and* for any other kind of preaching. Although several of these matters have already been mentioned in these pages, I want to mention them briefly in this context. I call them "pointers in telling a story." Some refer to the preparation phase and some to the delivery phase of our sermonic work.

1) *Attend to every "insignificant" line.* Our choice of biblical narratives probably will be restricted to the more familiar stories— drawn often from the parables of Jesus. For this reason we are apt to concentrate on the familiar salient points in the story. This tendency will produce the obvious well-worn result of an ordinary message, while what is needed is a fresh angle of view. The unique slant can be facilitated by noticing what everyone else misses. In the Prodigal Son story as illustrated before, this unique angle hap-

pened by my concentrating upon one sentence which everyone seems to pass by. Most tellers of this story get the elder brother in from the field and immediately move to his conversation with his father—obviously an important encounter. But a closer look at the fact that he summoned a servant over to him will alert the reader who can momentarily forget the end of the story that it was a most peculiar thing for him to do. Likewise the fact that Nicodemus "came by night" to visit Jesus is a telling fact, although we are anxious to move on to the "important" lines of the narrative. Attend to every "insignificant" line.

2) *Look between the lines*. Much happens by way of context that often is missed by our attention to what is being said in a passage. By attending to the cultural context, for example, we may discover that which makes the story unique. Sometimes what *isn't* said is exceptionally important. For example, when Jesus was being tested by means of an inquiry about paying taxes to Caesar, he never did answer the question of what belongs to whom. What he did was to embarrass and undermine the questioner who wound up revealing that he was in the wrong place with a Roman coin. The punch line to the story of the talents—with Jesus saying "to every one who has will more be given, and he will have abundance; but from him who has not, even what he has will be taken away" (Matt. 25:29)—seems a hard, almost cruel line as long as we project the concept of *profit* into a story about slaves, who do not get a percent of the gross, and hence whose "abundance" is something else altogether. Look between the lines.

3) *Catch every encounter*. Many biblical stories move exceptionally fast. It is even possible that their remembered form has been compressed from the original telling. In order to see deeply the picture being painted, often it is helpful to stop between the explicit actions long enough to imagine the implicit action. For instance, Zacchaeus was invited down out of the tree. We are told a bit about crowd reaction, and then are whisked away quickly to Zacchaeus' house. But wait a minute. What did Zacchaeus think and feel after Jesus addressed him and before he received him joyfully? How did he get out of the tree? And what did he and Jesus talk about as they walked to his home? The narrative doesn't say—

and we are given a chance for our imagination to paint the picture.
Later we can veto some of the results of our imagination (as being
contrary to content, context, etc.). But it is important to allow our
imagination to work *first*, and let our scholarship have veto power
second, rather than to work the other way around. He/she who goes
too quickly to the exegetical experts will become a poor story teller.
She/he who never goes to the exegetical experts will become an
irresponsible story teller. Although you will not actually use every
imagined scene in any narrative, those that are used will shed light
on the theme. Catch every encounter and imagine what the scene
must have been like.

4) *Bring data from your own experience.* Often we find it difficult to identify with a story's "villain"—who obviously is wrong,
immoral, etc. So the Prodigal Son generally is portrayed as a
rebellious teenager who flippantly tells his father that he wants to
"do his own thing." Likewise the elder son is painted as a stubborn
petulant one who never sins and never forgives. But have you ever
left home for *good* reason; or have you grown weary of special treatment given to the undeserving? If so you can enter the story with
empathy for both sons, and your hearers will join you there. If a
narrative contains events and material outside your experience,
imagine someone you know and respect who has had such experiences. By investment of yourself into the narrative, you are more
likely to do justice to the characters in the story.

5) *Move behind behavior to motive.* I have already indicated
how behavior tends to be either/or while motives are mixed and
fluid. The prodigal stays or leaves, but the cumulative reasons for
each may reveal only a slight edge of one over the other. The behavior of the Pharisee in the Pharisee and the publican narrative
appears on the surface so vain and self-serving as to make him *un*-
credible—a conclusion which is reason enough to ask if there are
not other motives at work. In the process of our looking for the
internal motives he will begin to look more and more like the rest
of us. The issue is not to find excuses for unethical or otherwise
inappropriate behavior, but to ascertain the causative factors in order to a) help the listeners identify with the character, and b) estab-
lish a credible context in which the gospel can be relevantly heard.

Move behind behavior to motives. A similar way of approaching the matter is to:

6) *Move behind facts to prior dynamics.* Facts like still shots of moving objects may prove helpful for close scrutiny but almost invariably distort the experiential reality. Whatever conclusion one may draw about the betrayal by Judas, it must be set within the context of his being a trusted and ongoing member of the group of disciples. Likewise, Jesus perceived more than immediately available facts when he came across the man at the pool of Bethsaida, and asked: "Do you want to be healed?" (John 5:6). While facts tend to set matters in a context of contradiction, an examination of the underlying dynamics generally will move apparent contradictions to the realm of ambiguities. Move behind facts to prior dynamics.

7) *Utilize the senses.* Jesus portrayed vividly the scene of the prodigal's homecoming party so that the elder son and the rest of us could hear the music, see the dancing and smell the food. Utilization of the senses in story telling is not a cheap device for "effect"; it is the entree to participation for the listener. We need to remember that the ear dominates the preaching context, unlike other aesthetic experiences like film or theater. It takes only a moment to depict a particular scene instead of reporting one. Utilize the senses.

8) *Switch identification.* "You know that the rulers of the Gentiles lord it over them, and their great men exercise authority over them" (Matt. 20:25), Jesus reminded the other disciples who were angered over the presumption of James and John. As long as we identify with Jesus and the five wise maidens waiting for the wedding to begin, the foolish ones receive little pity for their stupidity. But once we are in their shoes, the hurt of being kept out of the wedding feast changes altogether the existential dynamics of the judgment. This is not to say that the import of Jesus' story should be muted or distorted; it means only that it must be experienced *with the agony and grief included.* Judgment given is one thing; judgment received is altogether a different matter! New insights, fresh angles of view are possible by the simple method of switching identification.

9) *Utilize active grammer.* Jesus did not say: "It would be a

genuine act of environmental beneficence if the wind velocity were to be reduced through responsiveness to my desire." He said: "Peace! Be still!" (Mark 4:39). Passive and subjunctive verbs and prepositional phrases cut the life out of oral speech. No wonder the narratives of the Old Testament preach so easily. They are alive with strong nouns and active verbs. Otherwise abstract concepts often are put in narrative form: "But the Lord God called to the man, and said to him, 'where are you?'" (Gen. 3:9). Note the simplicity, boldness and action of language in this section from Jonah:

> And the LORD spoke to the fish, and it vomited out Jonah upon the dry land. Then the word of the LORD came to Jonah the second time, saying, "Arise, go to Nineveh, that great city, and proclaim to it the message that I tell you." So Jonah arose and went (Jonah 2:10–3:3a).

Utilize active grammar.

10) *Break into first and second person singular form.* The advice of John Ciardi and Miller Williams for aspiring fiction writers in *How does a Poem Mean?* is likewise good advice for us:

> A good novelist who wishes us to know a character does not tell us that character is good or bad and leave it at that. Rather, he introduces the character, shows him in action, and lets his actions speak for him. . . . One of the skills of a good poet is to enact his experiences, rather than to talk about having had them. "*Show* it, don't *tell* it" he says, "make it happen, don't talk about its happening."[9]

When Jesus had the prodigal son come to his senses, he could have noted that "the son decided to return home, confess his sin, and ask for a job." Rather, Jesus put it in first person singular language, and even included a dramatic monologue within the monologue:

> But when he came to himself he said, "How many of my father's hired servants have bread enough and to spare, but I perish here with hunger! I will arise and go to my father, and I will say to him, 'Father, I have sinned against heaven and before you; I am no longer worthy to be called your son; treat me as one of your hired servants.'" and he arose and came to his father (Luke 15:17–20a).

Break into first and second person singular language.

11) *Move from the subjective to the objective, from particular to general—and back again.* Life involves a constant flow between inner and outer realities and between the "small" particulars and the "large" generals. So should our storytelling. Wendell Johnson in *People In Quandaries* speaks of people who engage in what he calls "dead-level abstracting."[10] Typically they remain at one of the two poles of the continuum—either providing all eggs and no basket (low-level) or several baskets and no eggs (high-level). So the excited world traveler returns to relate all the minute details of leaving the European hotel room for a tour of the city on a particular day but we never learn what city nor what was the overall import of the experience. (My small children often make this kind of mistake in retelling the moment-by-moment details of a television show.) On the other hand, other returning travelers will describe eloquently the "awesomeness," "grandeur," and "utter beauty" of the Swiss Alps, but we do not receive enough specifics to know even what they actually look like. (My small children tell me that I often make this mistake—no doubt a vocational hazard.)

Note too, that in these descriptions of dead-level abstracting often another issue is involved—the failure to move from inner reality to outer reality, from subjective to objective, and back again. Stories need eggs and baskets, objective facts and subjective feelings.

12) *Set the stage (foreshadowing).* After a story's form is fairly complete in one's mind, it is time to review it for the purpose of foreshadowing major turns or events. This technique is one often utilized in other forms of story plots, and is not difficult to do, but is relatively unknown explicitly in the homiletical world. What "foreshadowing" means is that in order to highlight the importance of a later event, the story teller gives an earlier but then unrecognizable clue. When the later moment is reached in the process of the telling, it becomes highlighted by the prior remark. For example, in my telling of the prodigal son story, I want to emphasize the fact of estrangement between father and son prior to the pig pen scene. So I have the father look up and say to the son at the moment of departure: "Son, you're always welcome here. Don't forget who you are . . . and keep in touch, okay?" "Sure, Dad, I'll

be in touch." Then later when things begin to turn sour, he *doesn't* stay in touch—but not by choice exactly:

> He doesn't forget who he is; it simply becomes too painful to remember who he is. And to keep in touch now . . . well, would *you* want the folks at home to know where you spent last night—and with whom?

This latter portion of the narration is possible without the foreshadowing, but is enhanced by it. All one has to do is decide what is an important moment, and see if the stage can be set in a preceding moment.

The above-mentioned pointers are useful in any kind of preaching, but can be experimented with more easily when telling a biblical story. Central to our task—whether utilizing a biblical narrative or dealing with any other theme—are the dual concerns of maintaining the ambiguity necessary for sustaining interest and looking for the diagnostic reversal which will turn human experience upside down and hence make ready the context for the proclaimed Word to happen.

Tell the story!

# references

**Introduction:**

1. Michael Polanyi, *Knowing and Being* (Chicago: The University of Chicago Press, 1969), p. 133.

**Section One: The Sermon as Narrative**

1. Henry Grady Davis, *Design for Preaching* (Philadelphia: Fortress Press, 1958), p. 21.

2. Marshall McLuhan, *Understanding Media: The Extensions of Man* (New York: The New American Library, Inc., 1964), p. 88.

3. J. Samuel Bois, *The Art of Awareness* (Dubuque, Iowa: Wm. C. Brown Company Publishers, 1966), p. 16.

4. Benjamin J. Whorf, *Language, Thought and Reality*, cited by Bois, *The Art of Awareness* pp. 156–157.

5. Davis, *op. cit.*, p. 82.

6. Ilion T. Jones, *Principles and Practice of Preaching* (New York: Abingdon Press, 1956), pp. 87–102.

7. Fred B. Craddock, *As One Without Authority* (Enid, Oklahoma: The Phillips University Press, 1974), p. 56.

8. Davis, *op. cit.*, p. 21.

9. Davis, *op. cit.*, p. 15.

10. Craddock, *op. cit.*, p. 56.

11. Eliseo Vivas, *Creation and Discovery* (Chicago: Henry Regnery Co., 1955) p. 191.

12. *Ibid.*, p. 134.

13. *Ibid.*, p. 211.

14. Robert Roth, *Story and Reality* (Grand Rapids, Michigan: William B. Eerdmans Publishing Company, 1973), p. 38.

15. *Ibid.*, pp. 23–24.

16. *Ibid.*, p. 42.

17. G. William Jones, *The Innovator* (Nashville: Abingdon Press, 1962), p. 12.

18. *Ibid.*, pp. 11–12.

19. Davis, *op. cit.*, p. 22.

20. The statement may be a paraphrase of his quotation of the editor of *The Christian Pulpit* in *The Word God Sent* (New York: Harper & Row, Publishers, 1965), p. 4.

21. Foster-Harris, *The Basic Patterns of Plot* (Norman: University of Oklahoma Press, 1959), p. 12.

**Section Two: The Stages of the Homiletical Plot**

1. Erich Fromm, *Man For Himself* (Greenwich, Ct.: Fawcett Publications, 1947), p. 49.

2. Reinhold Niebuhr, *The Nature and Destiny of Man*, Vol. I (New York: Charles Schribner's Sons, 1941) p. 182.

3. John Dewey, *How We Think* (Boston: D. C. Heath & Co., Publishers, 1933) pp. 12–16.

4. Kurt Lewin, "Quasi-stationary Social Equilibria and the Problem of Permanent Change," in *The Planning of Change*, ed. by Bennis, Benne, and Chin (New York: Holt, Rinehart and Winston, 1961), pp. 235–238.

5. Robert Roth, *Story and Reality* (Grand Rapids, Michigan: William B. Eerdmans Publishing Company, 1973), pp. 25–26.

6. Helmut Thielicke, *The Waiting Father* (New York: Harper & Brothers, 1959), p. 17.

7. Harry Emerson Fosdick, *A Great Time to Be Alive* (New York: Harper & Brothers, 1944), p. 1

8. J. Wallace Hamilton, *The Thunder of Bare Feet* (Westwood, N. J.: Fleming H. Revell Company, 1964), p. 70.

9. Paul Scherer, *The Word God Sent* (New York: Harper & Row, Publishers, 1965), p. 169.

10. Ernest Fremont Tittle, *The Foolishness of Preaching* (New York: Henry Holt and Company, 1930), p. 63

11. Leslie D. Weatherhead, *When the Lamp Flickers* (New York: Abingdon Press, 1945), p. 13.

12. Phillips Brooks, *Twenty Sermons* (New York: E. P. Dutton & Company, 1887), p. 353.

13. David H. C. Read, *The Art of Living* (New York: Broadcasting and Film Commission, National Council of the Churches of Christ in the United States of America, 1960), p. 13.

14. Gerald Kennedy, "God's Good News" in *Great Preaching Today*, ed. by Alton M. Motter (New York: Harper & Brothers Publishers, 1955), p. 82.

15. *Ibid.*, p. 83.

16. Stuart Chase, *The Tyranny of Words* (New York: Harcourt, Brace and Company, 1938), p. 99.

17. Thielicke, *op. cit.*, p. 126.

18. *Ibid.*

19. *Ibid*, p. 127.

20. *Ibid.*, p. 131.

21. Foster-Harris, *The Basic Patterns of Plot* (Norman: University of Oklahoma Press, 1959), p. 6.

22. Frederick Buechner, *Telling the Truth: The Gospel as Tragedy, Comedy and* Fairy Tale (San Francisco: Harper & Row, Publishers, 1977), p. 4.

23. As told by my colleague, George Baldwin.

24. Fred B. Craddock, *As One Without Authority* (Enid, Oklahoma: The Phillips University Press, 1974), p. 62.

25. William J. J. Gordon, *Synectics* (New York: Harper & Row, Publishers, 1961).

26. Foster-Harris. *op. cit.*, p. 12.

27. Thielicke, *op. cit.*, p. 28.

28. Paul Scherer, *Love is a Spendthrift* (New York: Harper & Brothers, Publishers, 1961), p. 85.

29. Craddock, *op. cit.*, p. 135.

30. Craddock, *op. cit.*, p. 139.

31. Craddock, *op. cit.*, p. 42.

32. Karl Barth, *The Word of God and the Word of Man* (New York: Harper & Brothers, Publishers, 1928), pp. 28–50.

33. Barth, *op. cit.*, p. 34.

34. Donald G. Miller, *Fire in Thy Mouth* (Nashville: Abingdon Press, 1954), p. 17.

35. Peter Taylor Forsyth, *Positive Preaching and the Modern Mind* (Grand Rapids: William B. Eerdmans Publishing Co., 1964), p. 5.

36. Harry Emerson Fosdick, *The Living of These Days* (New York: Harper & Brothers, Publishers, 1956), p. 95.

37. Paul Scherer, *The Word God Sent* (New York: Harper & Row, Publishers, 1965) p. 19.

38. *Ibid.*, p. 7.

39. Craddock. *op. cit.*, p. 46.

40. Ilion T. Jones, *The Principles and Practice of Preaching* (New York: Abingdon Press, 1956), p. 98.

41. Lewin, *op. cit.*

42. Lewin, *op. cit.*, p. 236

**Section Three: Other Considerations**

1. Fred B. Craddock, *As One Without Authority* (Enid, Oklahoma: The University Press, 1974), p. 153.

2. *Ibid.*, p. 145.

3. *Ibid.*, p. 158.

4. *Ibid.*, p. 146.

5. Foster-Harris, *The Basic Patterns of Plot* (Norman: University of Oklahoma Press, 1959), p. 18.

6. *Ibid.*

7. *Ibid.*

8. Karl Barth, *The Preaching of the Gospel* (Philadelphia: The Westminster Press, 1963), p. 39.

9. John Ciardi and Miller Williams, *How Does a Poem Mean?* (Boston: Houghton Mifflin Company, 1975) p. 8.

10. Wendell Johnson, *People in Quandaries* (New York: Harper & Row, Publishers, 1946), pp. 270–276.